LOST BETV
Specter

* * * * * * *

by Roger Pretti

© 2012 by Roger Pretti

All Rights Reserved. No portion of this book shall be reproduced without permission of the author. This excludes brief citations used for research purposes, reviews or articles. Please direct inquiries to:

info@LEADVILLEGHOSTS.com

ISBN # 978-0-9838119-0-9

Cover illustration courtesy of Denver Public Library Western History Collection, # Z-2525

First Edition, Printed in the United States of America by AlphaGraphics, Inc.

- Chestnut St.-1879

Perched on the shoulder of the Mosquito Range, early-day Leadville was a beacon of light in a dark expanse of Central Colorado wilderness. It welcomed all comers, from the clever to the curious, to sample its brand of humanity. For the spirits of the dead, it was a home on the range.
–Denver Public Library Western History Collection, X-6373

* * * * * * *

"*Never did rat squeak behind the wainscot or rain drip upon the attic floor without a wild thrill shooting through me at the thought that at last I had come across the traces of some unquiet soul.*"

— Sir Arthur Conan Doyle,
The Secret of Gorelsthorpe Grange

* * * * * * *

CHICKEN HILL PUBLISHING

TABLE OF CONTENTS

INTRODUCTION 1

CHAPTER ONE---EARLY-DAY EERINESS 7
Midnight mystery on the Mosquito Road—A nickel or two—Corpse candle capers—Unsettled score turns tragic—'What's the matter?'

CHAPTER TWO---PHANTOMS OF THE MOSQUITO RANGE 23
Hoodoo on the high road—Wet footprints from a watery grave—Went to eternity in a winze—'Very distinct in the moonlight'—Terrible tales from Canterbury Hill—In the hollow moaning of the winds—Who killed "Crummy" Bill?—Shades on the streets of Adelaide—May I pick your brain?

CHAPTER THREE---SPECTRAL VICTIMS OF MURDER 47
Surreal sights on Brooklyn Heights—One ounce of lead—'I'm dead'—Rathway's specter—Slain behind the Saddle Rock—Gold, greed and the gallows—'You thought I was dead'—Murdered in Room 13

CHAPTER FOUR---GHOSTS IN THE GRAVEYARD, ETC 89
Requiescat In Pace—'Can't an old lady celebrate?'—Paddy plunges into the pit—Frightful sight at Albright's—Ghost in the bottles—'Dead enough'—Lurid lyrics at the Liberty Bell—Blind man's bliss—Ghostly messenger from Gotham

CHAPTER FIVE---SHADES OF THE RAILROAD GRADES 109
Midsummer mayhem on the Midland—Under the table and over the rail—Tragedy on the trestle—Beware The Boulevard—Maudlin on the main line—Lunar larceny—Wronged by the wheelright

CHAPTER SIX---SPIRITS IN THE SHADOW OF MT. MASSIVE . 123
A proper welcome—'Ye Mining Expert'—Necktie party's grim ghost—Death beneath the divide—Stone-dead at St. Kevin

CHAPTER SEVEN---UNDERGROUND APPARITIONS 137
Ghostly grit from the Morning Star—'Fiendish pandemonium'—Lost his head but didn't stay dead—Fred's First National grievance—The Penrose Ghost—Missed hole at the Moyer—Mr. Gallagher's ghost

CHAPTER EIGHT---URBAN HAUNTS 167
Leadville's haunted hill—'Too green to burn'—Phantom pilfers a sparkler—State-Street spiritualism—Witches and vampires in the mountains—Dark deeds at The Brass Bonnet—Miner Bill comes to call—Nymphs from the netherworld—When the clock struck three—No believer in hoodoos—Bones in the cellar—'Repent or die'—Phantom manipulation—October 1889—'Occasional strange things'—'String me up and whip me'

GLOSSARY OF MINING TERMS 215

BIBLIOGRAPHY 217

INTRODUCTION

Leadville's spectral side is never far away, and multitudes of the town's departed citizenry still frequent their earthly haunts, even those who gained immortality during the earliest days of the silver camp. Thousands of former residents were consigned to the grave beneath balsamic pines in local cemeteries, but mines, railroad grades, homes, businesses, vacant lots and long-disappeared ghost towns often have the reputation of being spook-ridden. In the thin atmosphere of the Carbonate City, restless souls are as common as the alpine grass.

Shades of the Leadville departed come in many forms and make their presence known in mostly subtle, but sometimes boisterous ways. Like the faint rustling of autumn leaves or the wind sighing among pine trees, some spirits of the netherworld are dim and shadowy. They can reveal their mysterious presence with a melancholy sigh, the lissome caress of ice-cold fingers or telltale rappings on a door or wall. Other restless spirits freeze blood in veins with shrieks in the night or a chilly hand placed on an unsuspecting shoulder. With the exception of the occasional black shadow seen out of the corner of our eye or the fleeting nighttime flicker of an apparition from the nether realm, most of the rest simply visit us in our dreams.

Violent deaths were an everyday occurrence in Victorian Leadville, and mining, ore processing and the railroad all did their share to reduce the population.

"The only thing really cheap here is dying," wrote a newspaper reporter from Ouray in 1879 following his visit to Leadville. "Just go down to the Sweet Canaan faro rooms and tell the party there that you want to whip somebody and the thing is done. No doctor's bills to pay, no medicine, no pain, no weeping relations, and—no funeral! The sexton takes you home and sends a bill to the coroner—'To plantin' one foot, sixty cents.' That's all of it."

Hundreds of former Leadvillites were whisked out of this life and into the next world without a moment's notice, and certain souls likely were caught between the familiarities of mortal life and the mysteries of the realm beyond. Imprisoned between the here and the hereafter, some surely chose to cling to the mundane and remain in Leadville in spirit form. For these denizens of the silver camp, a single mortal lifetime probably wasn't long enough to enjoy the city's wickedness or reap the benefits it had to offer. Others, snatched from life in the grip of consumption, pneumonia and other maladies of the day, joined their ancestors in less dramatic ways, but their share of the spirit population walks among us as well.

Unsettled claims of love and jealousy obliged some Leadville ghosts to return in search of a paramour's affection. Homicide victims, caught in the confusion of a sudden, emotional demise, often reappeared to the living in order to provide clues to an unsolved crime. Many a departed miner continued working the claim or returned as a benefactor for his companions, warning them of dangers lurking on the next level or just around a bend in the drift.

Whatever the reasons that compelled Leadville's dead to linger among the living, otherworldly visitations still remain a matter of speculation. Some spirits might be eternally attached to people, places or events. Others, hesitant to leave their alpine abode, continued searching for wealth in mines or businesses, at the poker tables or along busy thoroughfares. Surrounding Leadville, the high, lonely peaks of the Upper Arkansas Valley provided an ideal atmosphere for restless souls who perished there—an echoless place to eternally re-enact the drama surrounding the death of their mortal bodies.

In local burying grounds, the life force emanating from bones in coffins might be enough to generate apparitions of the dead, while violent summer electrical storms and ionized solar winds sweeping past earth could create the charged atmosphere favorable for ghosts to materialize. Limestone rock formations bathed in acidic water and honeycombed by underground mine workings make up a carbonate witch's brew that might also precipitate paranormal activity in the Leadville area.

"Haunted houses are plentiful enough over the country, but Leadville has something in the ghostly and supernatural line which goes a haunted house one better," said a newspaperman in 1900, after unearthly visitors infested the Mikado mine.

Hidden mineral riches were the objective of the early seekers of wealth in Lake County, and the mines provided a flawless ambience for ghostly encounters, real or imagined. The dank galleries, meandering drifts, open winzes, eerie stopes and seemingly bottomless shafts of the diggings presented a hazardous and otherworldly atmosphere. Perfect darkness, pierced only by the pale light of miners' candles and coupled with the rumbling of ore cars, echoing voices and laughter, the sounds of picks, hammers, groaning timbers and dripping water were enough to stir the most skeptical imagination. Add to this, the miners' recollection of fatal accidents in the workings, and the macabre portrait of the Plutonian environment in which they worked was complete.

Legends surrounding the dead and their return to earth accompanied immigrant miners from Europe, and these tales populated the Leadville worksite with all manner of phantoms and sprites.

"No mine is free from the spectral visitors, I have heard, after some fatal 'cave-in' or fall from the hoisting bucket has occurred and some unfortunate comrade given a lighter 'shift' or a higher 'property,'" said an early Leadville newsman.

Centuries of mining in Wales, Cornwall and the North of England gave rise to beliefs in diminutive creatures that inhabited underground crevices and fissures in the mines. These unpredictable elf-like beings with long, hooked noses and pointed ears came across the Atlantic in the miners' grub buckets and found their way to the goldfields of the Rockies. Once on American soil, they became known as Tommyknockers.

Often believed to be the spirits of dead miners, Tommyknockers rarely were seen, but made their presence known in other ways. Tapping from within rock walls, they could be heard secretly working their own rich veins of ore. Rapping on timbers or iron pipes, they guided miners along drifts and warned them of rock falls or other imminent dangers. Their less benevolent side could result in endless vexation for any miner who doubted their existence, and provoking these beings by whistling underground was to invite disaster.

Among other deviltries, they were known to hide tools

or lunch buckets, kick out the rungs of ladders, clip miners' suspenders, blow out candles or hurl rocks at passing men. After snuffing out a candle, the sprite would re-kindle the flame just before a miner put his lighted match to the wick. As soon as the man dropped the matches into his pocket, the gremlin would extinguish the light again in typical impish fashion. The torment would continue until the invisible prankster lost interest or found something else to attract his attention.

"As every experienced hardrock miner knows, it's the tommyknockers that make the mine-cars jump off the rails," said Fisher Vane in a 1937 issue of the *Mining Journal*. "And the same ornery little devils pack off the tools that you well know you laid right there beside the track on the 700 level, 50 paces back from the face…but where the heck you'll find that pet pick, with the new handle Bill, the blacksmith, just put into it for you, only the tommyknockers know!"

Despite their ability to aggravate, the presence of these strange beings in a mine was considered lucky, and workers often left food, tobacco or other small gratuities in order to stay on the good side of their mysterious companions. Many miners who escaped accidents with their lives credited their good fortune to the benevolent spirits that inhabited the depths.

Sometimes, what seemed like an irksome Tommyknocker prank turned out to be a stroke of fortune, as one Colorado miner realized while standing atop a rock protruding from a pool of water in an underground cavern. Suddenly, he felt himself pushed from behind by unseen hands, the victim of a shove that launched him off his perch and into the drink. Angry and soaking wet, he made his way to dry ground just as a huge boulder fell onto the spot where he was standing moments before.

Sadly, with the advent of modern technology in the mining industry, the Knockers were obliged to retreat deeper into the pitch-dark solitude of completely abandoned workings.

"Back in the dear dead days of the skewer candlestick and the old reliable Standard Oil candle the little devils were bolder than they are nowadays," Vane continued. "These new-fangled carbide mine lamps never did sit well with the tommyknockers.

Too much like the dreaded light of day."

Miners' heads, generally hidden beneath leather slouch hats, were inviting targets for the invisible imps that populated the dimly-lit workings.

"Before bakelite bonnets blossomed into the mining scene, I've had many a little rock bounced off my cranium when I knew positively that it had been deftly dropped by some little devil of a tommyknocker," Vane said, adding that drillers also were the victims of their otherworldly pranks.

"When good sharp hand-steel 'fitchered' in the hole, the hardrocker behind the singlejack knew what was to blame."

Even after the advent of air drills, the diminutive saboteurs quickly became adept at silencing the insufferable machines, whose roar was enough to make a preacher swear. After all, the new drills completely drowned out the sound of the Tommyknockers' own mysterious rappings.

Like most lingering shades of the departed, Leadville's ghosts were gifted with endless patience and a willingness to work very hard for the slightest morsel of recognition from their largely unperceptive mortal counterparts. When interviewed on the topic, the phantom in Mark Twain's *A Ghost Story*, gave his otherworldly opinion on the matter.

"I felt that if I ever got a hearing, I must succeed for I had the most efficient company that perdition could furnish. Night after night we have shivered around through these mildewed walls, dragging chains, groaning, whispering, tramping up and down stairs, till, to tell you the truth, I am almost worn out."

What follows are some of the early romantic ghost tales from the valley, canyons and ranges of Lake County's splendid mountain environs. Launched out of Leadville and into the immortal realm, these pioneers were numbered among the dead, but their spirits were compelled to remain in the alpine atmosphere for awhile, or perhaps eternity.

- Evergreen Cemetery

CHAPTER ONE
EARLY-DAY EERINESS

- Pack train on Mosquito Pass in the 1880s
Mules, and their first cousin the burro, have a long history of freighting goods in the Rocky Mountains. This 1880 pack train of longears, one wearing a pair of doors like wings, is on the Alma side of the Mosquito Pass trail.
–Denver Public Library Western History Collection, X-21769

MIDNIGHT MYSTERY ON THE MOSQUITO ROAD

Listening attentively to several world travelers talking over drinks at a Leadville public house one winter evening in 1887, a patron asked a newspaper reporter if he believed in ghosts.

"No," was the laconic reply from the scribe, who had written about everything from astrology to zoology during his career. "Well, if you care to take a seven-mile ride with me," the traveler said. "I will show you something that will disabuse your mind of these fallacies. Just come and get in my buggy and we'll go."

Always ready entertain a new angle on life in the Carbonate City, the reporter wasted no time accepting the invitation, even if it meant a mild case of frostbite. It was around midnight when the two stepped out of the tavern, boarded the hack and drove up East Sixth Street. Passing through Evansville, they entered the timberline expanse of Big Evans Gulch and approached the Mosquito Range, a crystalline wall of Olympian proportions rising in front of them.

"The old toll gate was there but no grizzly-faced toll man appeared to collect the toll," the news story said of the jolting ride up the escarpment. Horse and driver maneuvered the treacherous switchbacks of the Mosquito Road to the top of the pass.

"The scene was truly beautiful," the writer continued. "The old moon was slowly rising in the east and was not yet visible in the valley, where the city, with its myriads of lights, its dance halls and its church spires was nestled beneath."

The hills were white with snow.

Presently, the driver spoke of the object of their journey to this bleak, lonely pass perched on top of the world.

"Twelve years ago an old man owned a jack-train that brought provisions into Leadville. It was before the railroad entered the high mountains. Everything was brought in by teams."

One day the old teamster didn't arrive as expected at his destination. Hearing of the disappearance, the clients who hired him to carry their goods suspected that an accident befell the man and a search party set out to find him. Near this isolated spot, said the buggy driver, freight man and burros were discovered frozen in the grasp of death, and it was here that the phantom procession appeared nightly making its way to Leadville.

Descending from the buggy, the two men walked a short distance down the road toward Mosquito Gulch. One-half hour later they stopped at a place where the trail sliced across the hill above them. The guide looked at his watch and said it was almost time for the supernatural sight to appear. The pair sat on boulders and said nothing while the traveling man quietly puffed on a cigar and waited.

"It seemed like a week to me, a cold wind having arisen," the reporter lamented. "I was almost frozen, and was wishing myself at home. Suddenly, my companion clutched me nervously by the arm and pointed to the trail. The sight I saw made each individual hair on my head stand on end. There on the trail, coming around a sharp angle created by a large boulder was a jack-train of twenty-three animals. They all emitted a faint phosphorescent glow, which made them all the more vivid against the side of the hill."

Now and then, the last donkey would lean his load against a projecting rock to rest himself. The driver, walking behind, poked it with a short stick, whereupon it resumed its eternal march toward the carbonate camp. The specters of man and animals soon disappeared around the end of the hill leading to the summit of the pass.

Returning to the buggy for the trip back to civilization, the driver told the reporter this apparition could be seen on any dark night.

Meanwhile, back in Leadville, wandering spectral women in coal-black attire made a baleful impression on city residents.

* * * * * *

"Between the hours of 12 midnight and 1 a.m., despite the fact that all doors are securely fastened, an uncanny object, a man without a head enters all occupied rooms of the house and executes a dance, which although grotesque, is simply terrifying. Then a sound like the rushing of wind is heard, a dismal green-white light flashes, and the horrible visitation disappears."

—Silverton Standard, May 25, 1907

* * * * * *

A NICKEL OR TWO

During an age when ghosts and specters flew thick and fast on the mountain wind, the appearance of an uncanny woman dressed entirely in black stalking the business district on State, Chestnut and Harrison unnerved superstitious townsfolk in February 1880. She was the first of several mysterious raven-like females to ply the streets of the city during Victorian times.

Besides her wandering habit, the funereal color of her clothing and pale complexion, she appeared to be a well-dressed and respectable ghost. The strange woman was completely out of place in the vice-ridden portion of Leadville, and her daily wanderings took her along streets lined with gambling resorts, dance halls, variety theaters, saloons and brothels. Most residents avoided the stranger at all costs, believing she was an errant soul on a mission from beyond the grave.

The newspaper of the day was less spiritual in its speculation about the wraith-like wayfarer.

"She is evidently a young widow, and rumor has it that she was left well-off, but has been defrauded and is now penniless and a stranger in a wild though hospitable city."

When asking for charity, the mystery woman merely said, "Will you give me a nickel or two? I need them."

Any money she received, she took to the nearest bakery or grocery and purchased her immediate necessities before disappearing. Whether ghost or living being, her identity or how she came to haunt the streets of Leadville remains a mystery.

While the woman in black was busy sending chills up and down Leadville spines, other specters took up residence in the wilderness south of the city, following prospectors as they picked and panned their way up the valley named after the "Hawkeye State".

* * * * * * *

"And Yonder shines Aurora's harbinger;
At whose approach, ghosts, wandering
Here and there, Tramp home to church-yards: damned spirits all."

—William Shakespeare, A Midsummer Night's Dream

* * * * * * *

CORPSE-CANDLE CAPERS

During the early days of the silver camp, ghostly goings on shivered their way into Iowa Gulch the day a pair of unemployed Nevada miners shuffled into Leadville's fashionable Clarendon Hotel restaurant and sat down to breakfast.

Alec Decker and Joe Colvin left Virginia City three weeks earlier, after their vein pinched out in the Sierras and they were lured to Colorado with news of the recent strikes at Leadville. Taking lodgings at the Clarendon, the pair discussed how best to begin their argentiferous adventure in the Carbonate Camp.

One morning, as they languished over their steak and flapjack repast, an easterner at the next table named Watkins overheard their conversation. A recent arrival to Leadville himself, he had some money to invest in mining but was unsure how or where to begin. He struck up a conversation with the two miners and before long a deal was struck in which Watkins agreed to grubstake Colvin and Decker in exchange for their prospecting experience. When paying ore was discovered, the capitalist would take fifty percent of the profits and the miners would split the remaining half between them.

That afternoon, the prospectors generously outfitted themselves with the necessary supplies and meandered over Rock Hill into Iowa Gulch. Within a few days they located a promising claim, threw up a cabin and began driving a drift into Long and Derry Hill. When they struck a rich vein, they concocted a scheme to get rid of their financier and pocket the profits themselves. Since neither miner was a desperado, murder was out of the question and after some deliberation, the pair finally hit on a plan to divest themselves of their unwanted partner.

One October morning when the trio entered the mine, they were mystified to discover a lighted candle perched on a rock near the breast of the drift. Trying their best to appear superstitious in the company of their East-Coast companion, the Nevada miners said the burning candle was a sinister omen. Leaving the tunnel after a day's work, the men returned next morning to find the eerie candle glowing in the same spot. This time the pair told Watkins they suspected it was the work of some disembodied spirit warning them of impending disaster. That night, the men decided to stand watch at the mouth of the tunnel in order to catch the phantom candle-lighter in the act. At 2 a.m., they cautiously wandered into the mine and found no lighted tallow, and in the company of a bottle of whiskey, sat down to guard the entrance until daylight, the miners regaling Watkins with weird tales of mine spooks and other uncanny superstitions. During the pre-dawn hours, Watkins dozed off, and as the sun crept over the Mosquito Range, the men entered the mine and once again found the lighted candlestick wedged into a crevice.

In the miner's world, calamity was strongly associated with anything three-up, and after the third appearance of the phantom taper, Colvin and Decker announced to Watkins their intention to abandon the spook-infested claim rather than set foot inside the tunnel again and face certain disaster.

"The prospect of having to stay alone with a ghost which was able to light candles did not appeal to the nerves of the young tenderfoot, and the result was that all three abandoned the property," reported a local daily in 1900.

Back in Leadville, the Nevada miners found a prospective buyer, took him to Iowa Gulch and showed him the mine. Accepting his offer of $10,000 with a 20 percent cash down payment, they returned to Watkins with the $2,000, saying it was a good price for a worthless and haunted mine. With $1,000 in his pocket, the Easterner left town. Decker and Colvin split the remainder and later received the balance of $8000 for their spook-ridden lode.

In the meantime, one mile up the gulch from Leadville, the decaying ghost of Oro City placer camp was home to silver miners of the hard-rock variety, but the pioneer spirits of the Gold Rush lingered like tobacco smoke on the air and whiskey on the palate.

* * * * * * *

- "Placer Mining in a Gulch" (The Illustrated London News)

"It is not strange that California Gulch with its peculiar history and romantic legends contains its quota of haunted cabins, mines and placer mines. The hills and mountains are filled with ghosts, goblins and faeries of good and evil, as many a toiler, prospector and old-timer will tell you with evident satisfaction."
—Leadville, Daily & Evening Chronicle, May 6, 1889

* * * * * * *

UNSETTLED SCORE TURNS TRAGIC

Soon after the gold discoveries in 1860, there was a general scurry of humanity to California Gulch. The day after the first prospectors arrived, 70 newcomers drifted in from the Arkansas Valley. Between April and July of that year, there were ten thousand people in the fledgling camp called Bough Town or Oro, at that time one long, drawn-out mostly tent city alongside the stream. By summer, 339 claims, each 100 ft. wide, were located along the five-mile length of the creek in that vast, high-altitude wilderness. Most prospectors daily washed out between $10 and $25 in gold from the gravel that lined the gully. As their reward following several months of labor at stream's edge, the most ambitious miners took out more than $80,000 in dust and nuggets. Early settlers Sam Kellog and Horace Tabor wrested a mere $75,000 from their claims in a six-day period.

In 1861, California Gulch was the most populous spot in

Colorado Territory. Most recent arrivals parked their wagons on the flattest piece of ground available, piled their grub and dishes underneath and slept inside. After prospecting, Three-Card Monte was the most profitable game in camp.

After three or four years and an equal number of washings and re-washings of the stream gravels, the population of the California Gulch dwindled to hundreds, and by 1874 the grand little gully was almost deserted except for its ghosts. During that year, Stevens and Wood located silver-bearing carbonates in the walls of the narrow ravine, a discovery that would entice thousands more to delve beneath the earth for the unexplored bedrock bonanza the district held.

During the erstwhile years of the camp, no money changed hands during business transactions, only gold dust, and riches sometimes were found literally underfoot, such as the day Oro City's great bough-covered, 150-foot by 75-foot log gambling hall was razed and $2,000 in gold dust was panned out of the dirt beneath the floorboards.

Among the early arrivals to Oro City was Dan Howard, known locally as "Big Dan", an exile from his hometown who came west to the new camp with little more than whiskey, tobacco and a change of clothes.

With an eye for pocketing his share of the nuggets without getting dirty, Dan put up a log and canvas cabin, and every night hosted gambling, drinking and dancing for the most notorious immigrants to Oro City. So violent was the place that Dan built the bar to the height of the customer's chin to serve as a kind of fortification behind which he could take refuge when bullets and other objects flew. Tables, scattered helter-skelter on the crude floor, were populated with the camp's most unsavory characters. In the rear of the house was a canvas-covered dance hall, where dozens of grimy men and a handful of abandoned women danced nightly to the tune of the fiddle and triangle. Dan called his place "The Empire."

* * * * * * *

Early-Day Eeriness

Big Dan, proprietor of "The Empire" offered up the best that lonely prospectors to California Gulch could hope for in exchange for gold. As fate would have it, he also provided the slab and tent city with its first female ghost.
–Image courtesy of History Colorado Photograph Collection. #10038245

* * * * * * *

In the summer of 1861, a young stranger walked into the tavern and gazed around the room as if searching for someone. His eyes landed on Dan, who was busy mixing potions behind the counter. When the bartender looked up and noticed the man standing in the corner, Dan dropped the bottle he was holding and began to tremble in his boots. Nervously, he went back to work, stealing an occasional look and trying to resurrect the vaguely familiar face from his memory. The stranger sat down at one of the gaming tables and never took his eyes off the man behind the bar.

From that moment, everything went wrong for Dan; he dropped glasses and bottles, served up the wrong spirits and snarled at customers. When he could no longer take the stranger's penetrating stare, the proprietor motioned to the young man to join him outside.

It was never fully known what happened in the darkness of the gulch but saloon patrons heard several gunshots followed by a shriek, after which Dan returned with an excited look in his eyes and blood on his shirt. He closed the bar, threw out the customers and bolted the door.

The next morning, a pair of miners on their way to a claim found the body of the stranger with bullet holes in the head and heart. When they opened the shirt to examine the wound, they discovered the corpse was that of a woman. Residents mounted a search to locate the suspiciously absent barkeep.

A letter, found in the stranger's shirt pocket and written in a woman's hand told how Dan lured the young woman away from loving parents with smooth talk and promises. She ran away with him, but soon he deserted her. Unable to return home and face the disowning wrath her mother and father, she went to a large city and lived hand-to-mouth. When the child was born, she placed it in an orphanage and continued west to the goldfields. Traveling from camp to camp in search of the man responsible for her downfall, she always carried a letter in her pocket. It said that if she were killed when they finally met, her spirit would return to haunt him forever.

Dan disappeared—he apparently packed a few necessities and left the gulch during the night.

Several days after the murder, a group of miners wandered up the gulch at midnight, and passing The Empire, they were aghast to see an unearthly glow containing the shapes of two men. The larger of the two pulled out a pistol and shot the other. A scream followed and the scene dissolved into darkness.

Opening under new management, eerie recollections of the murder dominated the conversations of The Empire's customers. In the weeks following the grisly deed, patrons of the saloon regularly witnessed the ghost of the young stranger glide into the room around midnight, take a seat in the corner, and after staring at the bar for a few minutes, disappear through the doorway. The spectral visits were so disturbing that bar customers eventually drifted away, and the rough building, once the scene of so much reckless revelry, soon fell into disrepair and stood empty beside the gulch road.

Early-Day Eeriness

- California Gulch-1873
With its supply of nuggets depleted, the pioneers to California Gulch extinguished the lanterns, closed the doors and left the keys of the narrow gully with the supernatural residents who still call the place home.
–Denver Public Library Western History Collection, X-10002597

* * * * * * *

Years came and went and Dan, wanted more dead than alive, eventually met the Grim Destroyer in a hail of bullets on the New Mexico border. The details of his violent demise revealed a transcendental twist following the killing of a recluse named Herndon, who lived alone in a log cabin in southern Colorado.

One afternoon, a traveler stopped to rest his mount at Herndon's place, and except for some bloodstains on the cabin floor, the hermit was nowhere to be found. In the weeks following his disappearance, the place gained the reputation of being haunted after a pair of belated wayfarers reported screams and uncanny lights in the deserted cabin. These were followed by the sound of a body hitting the floor. At the conclusion of the ghastly overture, the scene returned to darkness and silence.

Unaware of the place's unearthly notoriety, two pilgrims on

their way upstream noticed the place was still fitted with a stove and two crude bunks. They decided to spend the night there, and after supper, the men lit their pipes and indulged in a few stories. Near the climax of one tale, the candles sputtered and went dark, their feeble light being replaced by a spectral yellowish glow that filled the cabin. The pair saw a figure that appeared sitting on a chair in the middle of the floor. Presently, the door swung open and the form of a large man entered, walked up behind the seated one and struck him on the head with a piece of firewood. The victim fell from the chair, and his assailant removed something from the dead man's pocket, pulled up a few floorboards, dragged the corpse to the opening and forced it into the hole. The sojourners looked on in disbelief as the phantom killer replaced the boards and the eerie scene faded to blackness.

Dashing out the door, the travelers reluctantly took a light and re-entered the place to drag their beds outside. Sleep was impossible, but the next morning the men made an investigation of the cabin's interior, locating several loose floorboards where the body was placed during the previous night's vision. Removing the planks, they discovered a skeleton with a paper in its pocket identifying the remains as those of Herndon.

Big Dan, who terrorized the country for several years before the man's death, was suspected of the murder and a manhunt ensued. A party of armed searchers surprised Dan one morning as he stooped over a campfire making breakfast. Hearing a noise, the desperado arose quickly and drew his pistol, but before he could fire, he fell to the ground riddled with shot. He lived for about an hour, during which he confessed to murders as far away as California Gulch, and gave an exact description of the death of Herndon as witnessed by the travelers who saw the ghostly re-enactment of the crime.

After the murder was solved, Herndon's restless ghost no longer walked at the isolated cabin. However, following Big Dan's demise, midnight wayfarers through the gulch at Oro City still told of a shadowy form gliding through the cabin's sagging entrance, only to emerge a few minutes later and disappear. So frequent were the manifestations that those familiar with the tragedy steered clear of the spook-infested place, even during daylight hours.

"Ghosts? There were regiments of them! Where there had once been light and gayety and the music of dancing feet, there were now silence and death. But it was easy to see shadowy revels and hear the shuffle of feet that now lie at rest."
—Silverton Standard, March 14, 1896

* * * * * * *

'WHAT'S THE MATTER?'

Even as the mysterious woman in black was seeking her widow's mites along the byways of Leadville's commercial district, irksome apparitions of the gentlemanly variety vexed the occupants of an unpretentious rental cabin on Sixth Avenue below Harrison.

Montie Hernandez, husband of a New York actress who was scheduled to perform at Mr. Tabor's opera house, noticed the 'To Let' sign in the window of the bungalow and went to the landlord. Rental properties in 1880 Leadville were scarcer than hen's teeth and the prospective tenant wanted to know why the cabin was uninhabited.

"Them that's lived thar says th'place is spirit-haunted," replied the owner. "Two miners and a laundry man couldn't stay in it. I never saw nothin', but yous're welcome to go see for yerself."

Key in hand, Montie and his two housemates, all non-believers, went to search for spiritual manifestations at the humble cottage. When no ghosts materialized, the men signed the lease and moved in, Mr. Barbour and Henry Richmond taking the front bedroom and the Hernandez family living in the rear.

Peace and quiet prevailed for almost two months and the lodgers concluded that the ghosts were the wild imaginings of the previous tenants. Suddenly, the new residents fell victim to a series of unexplainable events.

Things took a supernatural twist one night when Mrs. Hernandez wasn't billed to perform. Placing her baby in the crib, she retired with the lamp still burning but awoke sometime later to the sound of voices in the room. Thinking it was her husband returning from the opera house, she scanned the chamber, saw the locked door and passed off the murmurings as sounds from the adjoining apartment.

Before long, Mr Hernandez and his companions arrived

and knocked loudly on the door. Entering the room, he noticed his wife's ornately decorated workbox on the floor, where it apparently fell or was thrown from its place on the mantle. She couldn't explain how it was flung down and smashed as she and the child slept.

While Montie spoke with his cabin mates outside, he heard his wife utter a hysterical scream. He ran in, pistol drawn, to find her gesturing toward the foot of the bed, where she said there was a strange man wearing a dark coat and hat standing next to the stove. A search of the entire room uncovered nothing, and as Mr. Hernandez looked under the bed, a second shriek startled him, causing him to strike his head violently against the frame. Cursing, he stood up and saw the woman pointing to the apparition again. Barbour and Richmond burst into laughter when Montie waved his pistol through the air, and his wife said his arm and gun passed through the vaporous body of the ghostly visitor.

"Who the hell are you and what the hell do you want?" Hernandez demanded of the invisible stranger.

At that, the woman said, the specter melted away and the occupants heard the report of a pistol outside the cabin and a voice saying "What's the matter?" Pistols in hand, the men threw open the door and were greeted by a corporeal police lieutenant and an opera house employee.

"Hold on," said the gendarme, looking down the barrels of three handguns. "Don't shoot!"

Unable to explain the origin of the mysterious gunshot, the policeman said that as he and his companion walked from the opera house three blocks away, a light flashed in their faces and a bullet whizzed past their heads, followed by the smell of powder smoke. No one else was in the area.

As the men searched the area around and between the cabins, a second shot rang out and Montie re-entered the house to check on his family. As the couple talked, the figure of the dark man appeared next to them politely asking once again "What's the matter?"

"Some s— of a b— has been playing funny business here and we're trying to find out who it is," Hernandez snarled.

Early-Day Eeriness

The phantom said nothing, turned and ambled away, followed closely by the men. As the group watched, the stranger reached the middle of Sixth Avenue and evaporated into the night air. Puzzled by what they witnessed and accompanied by a few ardent spirits of their own, the gentlemen attempted to unravel the mystery until dawn finally broke over the eastern range, with Mr. Hernandez vowing that he would make a ghost of anyone who bothered him or his family again.

* * * * * * *

"Mr. Farrel, who struck Meadow Lake, died a victim of remorse in one of the leading hospitals in San Francisco 'haunted by the spirits of 2,000 deluded pioneers and prospectors passing and repassing his dying bed.'"
—*White Pine Cone, July 16, 1886*

* * * * * * *

CHAPTER TWO
PHANTOMS OF THE MOSQUITO RANGE

Extending for a distance of some 40 lonely miles along the geographic center of the state, the frozen heights, circuitous trails and mineral riches of the Mosquito Range all did their part to help humankind solve the mysteries of the Great Beyond.

After prospectors located the gilded gravels of California Gulch, Mosquito Pass formed the high-set eastern gateway to the Upper Arkansas Valley. The trail between Fairplay and the diggings at Oro City gained and lost 3,000 ft, of elevation over its roughly 10-mile distance, and hundreds of pilgrims walked, braving the rocky switchbacks and the midwinter horrors of the precipitous western descent into Evans Gulch. Many who thought they could easily traverse the Mosquito trail to the goldfields died in the attempt.

Still visible today are scores of furrows sliced many years ago into the alpine sod by heavily loaded wagons crossing the crest of the divide.

Author Carl Akers speculated on the nature of the ghostly conjecture that still moans on Mosquito's bone-chilling wind.
"There must be lots of ghosts up there, on those high, cold peaks…up there on once treacherous Mosquito Pass where so many were killed or frozen to death trying to get to the other side. Those grubby, grinning old ghosts must be just sitting there, talking about the price of silver, and if goes up any further, some of the old mines will be reopened …and everybody knows, they'd say, there's more silver down there than was ever taken out."

* * * * * *

During the construction of the Colorado Midland railroad grade, an engineer reportedly chased a ghost along the track at a heavy curve west of Leadville. The driver recognized the phantom as one of the three men legally hanged near Evergreen Cemetery. At that time, stories circulated that the trio of executed felons had returned to Leadville to plague their enemies.

—*Condensed from a Leadville newspaper dated June, 1886*

* * * * * *

Phantoms of the Mosquito Range

Mosquito Pass, whose rockbound trail was once so busy, is still home to a few ethereal pilgrims who perished during the trek to and from the placers of California Gulch.

HOODOO ON THE HIGH ROAD

After the railroad reached Leadville in 1880, stagecoach, wagon and foot traffic no longer bottlenecked over Mosquito Pass. When roads into and out of Lake County were expanded and improved following the turn of the century, still only the most adventuresome explorers made the trip over the 13,185-foot trail. Bearing tales of the stony, harrowing descent to timberline, a few lucky travelers rolled into Alma or Leadville with strange stories about their experience atop the range after being caught there during a blusterous, icy summer storm.

Those who waited out the squall in the safety of their vehicles on Mosquito's crest sometimes told of a pair of enigmatic, dark-suited men who appeared from behind the windswept hill, walking slowly with hats pulled low, coat tails flying and shoulders dipped into the tempest. When invited to climb into a car to wait out the storm, the man in the lead, without looking or lifting his head, grumbled something about "important business" and "going on". Despite repeated offers of shelter, the relentless wind flung the words into the blizzard and the dark pair disappeared quickly from view, making their way toward Fairplay.

Speculating briefly on the encounter, motorists generally passed off the incident as only slightly odd before continuing their journey down the mountain in the wake of the passing storm. However, what they witnessed were the wheels of eternal justice serving up a purgatorial banquet for the lost souls of a pair of murderers who came to their journey's end on the Mosquito road many years earlier.

During the gold rush to California Gulch, freighting supplies and hauling passengers across Mosquito Pass was a wager against mortality, even during the brief summers astride the range. But during the winter months, the astute gambler always opted to court lady luck in the safety of some warm Leadville faro room rather than lay odds on a successful trip across the divide.

Such wisdom escaped an unsavory sporting man named Henry Thomas, whose judgment at the green felt table was almost as poor as his eye for the high-country weather. During the numbing winter of 1881, the howling wind and driving snow on the Mosquito road offered better stakes for him and his companion than the gathering storm of prosecution they faced in Leadville.

On the day in question, the pair wagered all afternoon and lost their shirts at Jeff Winnie's gambling hall. Becoming more sullen and cantankerous with each unlucky turn of the wheel or unfavorable toss of a card, Thomas finally flew into a rage when a fire-eating variety actress named Minnie Eugenie sat on his knee and tried to cheer him up. The seething man dealt the woman a savage blow, prostrating her on the floor, and his partner, adding his own insult to the injury, kicked her as she lay there unconscious and bleeding. One customer who witnessed the brutal assault gazed at the frail, motionless figure in the sawdust and then at Thomas before clamoring, "He has killed her!"

With a final terrified glance at the victim and a room full of angry patrons close on their heels, both assailants dashed through the rear door of the place and left the city. For the next two days, police and the public searched fruitlessly for the pair, leaving not a coal bin or outhouse unchecked.

On the afternoon of the third day, a miner named Gwynne came into town from Mosquito, saying that he crossed the divide and met two men traveling east, one of whom he recognized as Thomas. Seeing signs of a storm descending on the range, Gwynne advised the pair to go no further and return to Leadville.

"We have important business and must go on," the gambler replied.

There must be something wrong or you wouldn't even think of going, the miner told the two men.

"No, there ain't," was the shouted answer. "It's very important business."

With that, the hikers hurried on and were soon swallowed up by the dark clouds racing across the summit. Gwynne descended the road only a short distance when a ferocious snowstorm enshrouded the top of the pass. The fleeing men became lost and their names were added to the somber list of victims on Mosquito's highway of frozen death.

When Gwynne learned the particulars of the manhunt, he told police about his encounter with the fugitives. Despite several expeditions to the frostbitten heights, the killers weren't located until June when their frozen and mummified remains eroded out of a snow bank during the spring thaw. By the time their earthly remains were committed to the rocky ground at Evergreen, their restless spirits had long since embarked on their frigid, never-ending penance across Mosquito Pass.

* * * * * * *

"Tom says he hears the most strange sounds every night all about the cabin. Scarcely do they blow out the light and compose themselves to slumber, than they hear footsteps without the door and moanings and groanings that would make each separate hair to stand on end like the quills of the fretful porcupine, and the moment one of them gets up to investigate the noises cease. Tom says he has shot with his revolver through the door and cracks between the logs, in the direction of these sounds, until the cabin is like a sieve, but the impalpable ghost cares not for bullets."

—Rocky Mountain Sun, November 7, 1885

* * * * * * *

WET FOOTPRINTS FROM A WATERY GRAVE

Adelaide Park, located on the eastern flank of the Mosquito Range two miles east of Leadville, is a sylvan spot lying just north of the saddle between Iron and Yankee hills. At first glance there is little to remind visitors to this marshy glade that scores of residents once called this peaceful spot home. A closer inspection of the valley and surrounding forest reveals evidence of mining as well as foundations of homes and businesses that once occupied the site.

Concealed among the pines one hundred yards to the southwest is the Belgian Mine, the site of the district's worst mining accident in which six tunnelers were asphyxiated following an explosion of giant powder in September 1895.

North of the road, there rises a ridge of gravel and boulders, pushed to the side of Evans Gulch when a glacier filled that valley thousands of years ago. As the climate warmed and the frozen mass disappeared, pockets of ice lodged inside the ridge also melted, leaving the space they occupied to be filled with the surrounding earth. One such feature can be found in the forest north of Adelaide Park. When a large block of ice melted, it was near enough to the surface to form a crater-like depression 15 yards across and deep enough to hold a sizeable pond when filled with groundwater. At this spot, young Richard Barton passed through the portals of death, and it is here that an unearthly glow beneath the surface of the lagoon signaled his return to visit the friends and neighbors he knew in life.

Boys and rafts are living proof that pirates once roamed the high seas in search of adventure and plunder. Even in the settlement of Adelaide, young minds turned sticks into swords and rafts into pirate ships on the small lake.

One summer afternoon during the late 1880s, 10-year old Richard boarded a homemade raft and paddled to the center of the pond. He had no idea that the Grim Ferryman was about to carry him across the River of Death.

Mid-lagoon, the raft began to list, and the frightened boy jumped overboard, probably thinking he could touch the bottom and safely wade to shore. However, the water was deeper than he thought and the youngster was soon snatched away by the fingers of death. Barton's companions, sitting at the edge of the pool, saw their friend come to the surface five times before disappearing completely. They ran to where some men were working nearby and told them about the accident. One of the rescuers boarded the raft, made his way to the center of the lagoon and pulled the pale body from fifteen feet of water.

Following the drowning, parents advised their children to stay away from the lake. For the most part they obeyed, with the exception of a few of the older boys in town who were brave enough to gaze down at the dark water that claimed Richard's life.

One semi-warm evening in late July, two boys from Finntown passed the pond on their way home, and thinking it to be just another abandoned prospect hole, they paused to throw rocks into the water. A few minutes passed and they noticed a glow that seemed to emanate from the depths. It grew brighter, revealing the form of a young boy, motionless and suspended beneath the surface. Terrified, the pair made a headlong dash the half-mile distance to Finntown to tell their parents about the experience. In the company of several adults, they returned to the dark lake and found nothing out of the ordinary other than an extraordinarily somber atmosphere hanging over the place ahead of the gathering gloom.

Beginning that evening and continuing for many nights, several families with young children who were friends of the drowned boy reported strange but similar incidents at their homes. In each case, three knocks were heard at the door. When it was opened, the caller was nowhere to be seen, and the only evidence that someone stood on the doorstep were the wet prints of a small pair of shoes. Three of the residents reported seeing what appeared to be a dark figure, the size of a child, disappear around the end of the porch. Following the apparition to the side of the house, they found no one there.

Three miles southeast of Adelaide and 2,000 ft. higher on the range, the shade of a departed miner lingered in the perfect silence and darkness underground.

* * * * * * *

"We had supposed that the day of ghosts had passed, but we find ourselves mistaken. A few days since, Mr. Conles took a contract to sink shafts, etc., in the Saratoga Mine. He put in a gang of hands, and work began to go forward smoothly but presently there appeared a ghost. It was a headless man of moderate size. This caused great alarm, but presently the fright was increased by the appearance of a second ghost, that of a very large man, supposed to weigh two hundred and fifty or three hundred pounds. A few days since, a man was descending or ascending the ladder, when the man fell, receiving the injuries we reported a few days since. Since then the workmen have refused to enter the mine, and so work has been stopped. Such is the ghost sensation."
—Daily Register Call, March 15, 1868

* * * * * *

Phantoms of the Mosquito Range

- Continental Chief Mine
Secluded within the cold, mineral-rich depths of Mount Sherman, one dank drift among the maze of frozen workings of the old Continental Chief Mine hides a lamentable ghost story.

WENT TO ETERNITY IN A WINZE

Just below the crest of the Mosquito Range at an altitude of nearly 13,000 ft., the Continental Chief Mine reclines in the bottom of a high-altitude basin at the head of Iowa Gulch. Locked within its dismal galleries is a mining specter that endlessly re-enacts the final frantic moments of a life that ended with a death drop into a winze more than a century ago.

Miners at the Continental Chief around the turn of the 20th Century were familiar with the old workings of the mine, and they often passed through them during their labors. One deserted cavern was to be avoided at all cost, especially during the month of August, when the ghost of a dead miner returned to the stage where his life was extinguished in bygone days.

Over the years, the miners' uncanny sense of presences told workers walking along the dim tunnel they weren't alone as they passed the drift where Carlton Vold died. Most felt the specter's eyes gazing out at them from the darkness, and some even said they saw the wavering light from the candle he carried.

Old miners were in the habit of frightening their younger counterparts with stories of mine ghosts, and new employees often were sent into the fatal drift as an initiation rite during the first week in August, when the specter was said to appear. Many returned to their companions with tales of eerie sights and sounds, proof to the old hands that the place was indeed haunted.

Vold previously worked at the London Mine on the eastern side of Mosquito Pass but after losing his position there, he spent most of his spare time in Leadville tossing off drinks at Marty Muller's Saloon. Three weeks later, he found work at the Continental Chief, and reporting to his new employ, Vold was on the job only one hour before he fell into the jaws of death.

His first shift began at 10 p.m. when he and two other men started drilling the face of one of the lower drifts. Upon reaching the desired depth, hammering stopped and the men filled the holes with powder and spit the fuses. Horsetails of sparks arched across the drift like some Fourth of July pyrotechnic as the pair passed Vold on their way to safety. Telling him to hurry, the two miners trotted down the drift and took refuge around a bend. The new man got excited and in a rush to get away he forgot to light his fuse. Instead, Vold stood up and ran into a lateral drift at the end of which was a winze 30 ft. deep. Even though he was warned about the pit, he forgot its location and stepped into it. The muffled concussion of the blasts drowned out the man's shriek as he fell. When Vold's two companions returned, they found him lifeless with a broken neck at the bottom of the hole. Shortly after Vold's plunge into perdition, underground workers said they frequently heard the discarnate sounds of spitting fuses, footsteps and a sepulchral voice crying "Oh, my God!" coming from the fatal drift. Such strange sounds were common at the mine until its closure after World War I.

Phantoms of the Mosquito Range

- Clear Grit Mine

At a mine such as this, high on a timbered slope east of town, claim jumpers and mine guards engaged each other in a deadly battle in 1878. The tide of the fight finally turned in favor of the defenders, thanks to their ethereal comrades in arms.

* * * * * * *

"Are there masses that can be said for the repose of souls that are abroad such nights as this—spirits blown about by the viewless winds—coming in the storm and darkness with signs and portents, hints of memory and presages of doom?"

—Ambrose Bierce, Beyond the Wall

'VERY DISTINCT IN THE MOONLIGHT'

In the early years of the camp, ownership disputes were common and armed claim jumpers appropriated many mining properties either by threat or simply murdering the owner where he stood. Some attempted a more judicious approach, appearing at a cabin door with a legal looking paper—a ploy that produced mixed results. Other property owners relinquished their lodes at the prospect of a lengthy, expensive court battle.

For the most part, Leadville residents had little tolerance for lawbreakers, and tinhorn gamblers playing a crooked game always ran the risk of finding the muzzle of a self-acting six-shooter under their nose in less time than they could count three. "They have a habit of dealing promptly and severely with all kinds of swindlers and thieves anywhere in the mountain country," said an early writer known as Mack in his observations of life in the mining camp.

Claim jumpers ended up paying a high price when they chose to delve into the dishonest side of mining. In 1879, a man named Lavery resisted an attempt by lawmen to prevent him from stealing a property. Officer O'Connor shot him dead after the suspect pulled a pistol out of his pocket. Another rascal, Ed Frodsham, was locked up for the same offense later that year and tossed in a cell with Charles Stewart who was already in the bastile on assault charges. The Leadville citizenry, weary of the brazen methods employed by the town's criminal element, passed swift judgment on the pair that night.

"The beams of an unfinished house were compelled to bear fruit," said the Rocky Mountain News of the evening's events. "The tribunal of Judge Lynch has been established in our midst and two lives have been sacrificed at its pitiless command."

Dawn's early light crept over the Mosquito Range to reveal the dangling corpses of the two men. Pinned on Frodsham's coat, a handwritten warning named well-known thieves, lot jumpers, con men about town and even the city marshal that the midnight jury had a similar verdict awaiting them. So dire was the situation that the headlines of one Leadville newspaper read: 'Wanted—A Vigilante Committee.'

More fortunate lot-jumpers escaped with their lives but little else, according to an April 1879 issue of the New York Times. "Mingling with the stertorous rush of the saw mill and the horn of the night-braying donkey, the wakeful citizen may still occasionally hear the crash of breaking and falling timbers as the cabin of some 'jumper' is pulled to pieces by a crowd of men with horses, and the fragments dragged and strewn along the street for blocks, while the interloper escapes in a more or less primitive costume."

One of the more uncanny accounts involving a disputed claim took place east of the city in 1878.

"Yes, sir," a Leadville saloon patron remarked as he set his empty whiskey glass on the polished surface of the bar and gazed admiringly at himself in the mirror facing him. "I believe in ghosts, and what is more, always shall."

A small crowd gathered around the man after someone in the group asked if he ever saw a spook.

"Yes…I've seen several," he replied.

Saying that his experience was only a hallucination brought on by imbibing too much whiskey, the cynical bartender polished a glass and scoffed at the patron's words.

"It did not originate during a wild delirium caused by an excessive partaking of intoxicating beverages," said the gentleman as he bade the men accompany him out of earshot of the sardonic barkeep and into the next room to hear his story. Producing a long cheroot and lighting it, he kicked his feet up on a card table, glanced around with a self-satisfied smile and told the tale through a halo of smoke.

"It happened in Leadville early in 1878. The camp was being settled and there were lots of claim jumpers. The Flash Mine was brand new, showed promise and was 'spotted' by some unscrupulous scamps, who determined to 'purchase' the claim with revolvers, pistols and knives," the storyteller continued.

As a result, the owners hired eight men to watch the property against jumpers, but for several nights in a row, all was quiet and the guards thought the rascals gave up on acquiring the mine. As a result, the men relaxed their vigilance and their number dwindled down to one watcher while the rest stayed in the cabin playing cards.

On the evening in question, talk around the table was amiable, but hearing voices outside, the guards grabbed their guns and left the cabin to investigate.

They confronted nine lot jumpers who warned the defenders to get out if they valued their lives. The guardians answered with a volley of lead, and the jumpers returned the fire before retreating to a safer distance. After several more attacks, the dawn saw three of the eight guards left alive. Two were killed outright and three expired during the night from the effects of their wounds.

Several miles east of town and reinforcements, the mine guards had no choice but to stay and guard the claim lest the jumpers return and take over without a fight. The survivors carried the five dead men into the cabin, laying them shoulder-to-shoulder on the floor. The next day passed quietly, but at 8 p.m., a shot was heard and five claim jumpers appeared at the foot of the dump. Their rifle fire pinned the defenders to the ground, but to their surprise, they heard pistol shots coming from the cabin.

"I looked in that direction and saw a sight that has always remained unaccountable to me," the storyteller said as he struck a match and lit a cigarette. "There, coming out of the door, were all five of our comrades, whom we had supposed were killed in the melee the night before. I recognized them all, their features being very distinct in the moonlight."

They said nothing as they advanced toward the jumpers and drove them off. The phantom group then turned toward the cabin and entered. Two of the guards ran in after them and were astonished at what they saw.

"Lying on the floor in the same manner we had placed them, were the bodies of the five men," he told the listeners. "There was no life in any of them."

One member of the group of listeners in the saloon, a man with a green patch over one eye, questioned the events of that night.

"That is a harrowing tale indeed—and may I ask why you and your six comrades didn't keep inside the shaft house…and fire through the doors and windows, and…"

Having heard enough, the narrator gestured to the skeptic and told the group, "With the exception of this pre-Adamite individual, the gentlemen present will all step to the bar, and imbibe whatever they may each and individually perculiarize in the way of invigorating refreshment, at my expense."

* * * * * * *

"Deputy Sheriffs Smith and Korty say that the ghost of Frodsham, the lot-jumper who was hung by a committee of citizens years ago, and since that time is claimed to have been seen by many people in the sheriff's office at the court house, does not materialize as often as formerly."

—Leadville Daily Herald, February 5, 1885

* * * * * * *

TERRIBLE TALES FROM CANTERBURY HILL

In the summer of 1894, a lad named Sullivan was playing with several other youngsters on Canterbury Hill north of Leadville when their adventures took a hair-raising turn. They were exploring their way through a stand of timber when the leader of the group stopped and howled in terror. Panic-stricken, the boys saw the corpse of a man, body riddled with bullets, hanging from the limb of a tree. The group made a hasty retreat toward Leadville, splashing through Big Evans Creek and not stopping until they reached the El Paso Mine on the eastern city limits.

Stories concerning the Canterbury apparition circulated widely around town but none of the youngsters who saw came forward during the investigation that followed.

Three weeks later, a boy walked into the coroner's office with a similar tale. He gave a graphic description of the corpse he saw swinging in the wind. The mortician told him to get an adult, go to the place and see if the dead man was still suspended there. The young man never returned and no more reports of the hanging corpse surfaced.

"It may be possible that there may be a ghost on Canterbury Hill, just as in old England there was a ghost in the famous

Canterbury Lane," the press said of the mystery. "It is not likely that anyone would come to make the investigation."

While ghosts were busy hanging around on Canterbury Hill, the harping boreal wind funneling up Birdseye Gulch carried the mournful wails of the victims of a fire that consumed a boarding house there several years earlier.

* * * * * *

"It is in accord with the eternal fitness of things that ghosts should walk in the dead of the night."
—Mancos Times-Tribune, Jan. 3, 1919

* * * * * *

IN THE HOLLOW MOANING OF THE WINDS

Hidden above the valley of the Arkansas River north of Leadville, Birdseye Gulch tumbles down a precipitous gully from the Mosquito Range, slicing along the northeast side of Prospect Mountain and into the valley of the East Fork. Its upper end joins the Mosquito Pass road at timberline near the head of Big Evans Gulch.

Prospectors located placer diggings at Birdseye in 1876 and the development of the Gold Medal Mine and timber cutting for the charcoal industry brought the pioneers who founded the town of Howland near the mouth of the gulch. Three years later, the settlement was home to a post office and the 50 employees of the Birdseye Lumber Company, owned by Col. Henry Howland.

* * * * * *

- Gold Medal Mine- 1879
Birdseye Gulch, isolated from the carbonate excitements of Leadville, was the scene of high drama of the ghostly variety during the 19th Century.
–Denver Public Library Western History Collection, X-11003260

* * * * * * *

One evening during the winter of 1886, Leadville residents noticed an eerie glow illuminating the sky north of the city. Some thought it to be the Aurora Borealis, a rare but sometimes spectacular celestial event in the mountains. The next day, news reached town that it wasn't the Northern Lights, but the old sawmill boarding house in Birdseye Gulch that went up in flames during the night. Its occupants, Mrs. Brockway and her brood of three were not found following the conflagration and were believed to be consumed by the fire. In the wake of the blaze, stories of ghosts were on every tongue in the gully.

"The average man who had visited the blackened heaps of ashes was almost satisfied that the mother and three children had departed this life with the burning of the building and the superstitious often said to each other that in the hollow moaning of the winds that swept through the ribs of the gaunt pines they could hear the shriek of infants and the desperate cries of a woman," said a Leadville newsman in the wake of the fire. "This had been discussed so frequently that the belated prospector shuddered as he passed and whistled the imps that juggled their fire balls before him into the wilderness beyond."

Stout-hearted investigators dug into the scorched rubble without finding even the smallest fragment of human bone and came to the conclusion that the family was utterly incinerated.

Built in 1878, the Brockway's home originally served as the boarding house of the Birdseye Lumber Company and was the scene of years of strife between local prospectors and timber cutters. Seeing the forest and its potential supply of lumber disappearing before their eyes, the conflict took a serious turn when one cantankerous miner sent a pistol ball whizzing past the mill owner's head.

This display of force was effective and the teamsters abandoned the gulch, signaling the beginning of the end for the lumber business. Machinery was pulled from its moorings and the mill was put to the torch. Changing hands several times over the next few years, Mr. Brockway finally jumped the property, and with the exception of the boarding house, pulled down the remaining buildings with teams of horses and sold the logs for profit. He lost no time spending his ill-gained wealth at the local faro tables and skipped town, leaving his wife and children to their fiery fate. Insane in her final days, it was believed that Mrs. Brockway soaked the building in coal oil, inserted a piece of fuse and touched off the fire that illuminated their way to the next world.

Secluded and largely bereft of human habitation, Birdseye was regarded as a place to be avoided after sundown, when darkness closed around the gulch and shrieks of the dead carried on midnight zephyrs was the only sound to greet the ears of belated travelers.

While the Brockway sprites flitted around the upper reaches of Birdseye Gulch, the restive spirit of an 1880 murder victim hovered in limbo at his cabin near the railroad grade just uphill from Howland, where clues to an unsolved crime could be discovered.

WHO KILLED "CRUMMY" BILL?

"Crummy" Bill worked with the dirt haulers on the Denver & Rio Grande extension. No one knew his real name, only that he acquired his unusual moniker from the carpet of crumbs he always wore on his beard and woolen coat following meals. So plentiful were the bits of bread and cracker decorating his front side, that birds were known to land on him, pecking up the fallen morsels as he dozed in the morning sunshine on a bench outside the cabin door.

Like many men of the day, Bill didn't believe in banks and wasn't hesitant to show strangers the $300 in savings he carried in his coat for safekeeping. For this reason, he met an untimely end inside his hole-in-the-wall lodgings that clung to the mountainside just below the railroad grade at Birdseye. His body lay frozen and undiscovered for nearly two weeks until his troubled ghost finally caught the attention of a railroad worker who passed along the grade above Bill's former earthly abode.

Summoning all available atmospheric energy, Crummy Bill's specter finally flickered into the visible spectrum long enough to stop the passing man dead in his tracks. Pointing to his cabin 100 feet below, Bill turned, drifted across the snow and disappeared through the doorway of the shack. Making his way to the entrance, the workman peered inside and found a body under the broken down door. Brushing the drifted snow from the face of the corpse, he noticed the side of the skull crushed in, the result of a heavy blow. A gunshot wound to the forehead left no doubt that the unfortunate man was the victim of murder.

Hailing his comrades from their worksite further along the grade, the discoverer and his friends entered the cabin, scrutinized the pallid face and identified it as that of "Crummy" Bill, who disappeared on Thanksgiving Day. An investigation of the shanty revealed nothing but a wooden barrel for a chair, an old whiskey jug and a bed of pine boughs in one corner. Aside from a worn and empty money pouch and a plug of tobacco inside the dead man's coat, no clue to the crime ever came to light.

Bill took up new and slightly more cramped lodgings at Evergreen Cemetery, but his soul refused to rest, unhappy with the unfinished state of affairs back in the gulch. Even after more than 130 Decembers, his ghost still lingers, covered in phantom cracker crumbs, in the deep forest near the Birdseye rail crossing, eternally waiting for passersby who never come.

SHADES ON THE STREETS OF ADELAIDE

Some years later, another restless spirit roamed the town of Adelaide, two miles east of Leadville, where dinner table conversations among residents centered on a spectral visitor frequenting the streets of town nightly between 11 p.m. and 1 a.m.

Described as a luminous female form that crossed the park some distance from the Johnnytown Road, the spirit walked to one particular spot and lingered there for a time before evaporating into the night. Daylight investigations revealed that the place chosen by the specter was the abandoned and collapsed shaft of the St. Julia Mine. When interviewed about the origin of the ghost, one long-time resident recalled a tragedy that occurred there many years earlier.

When the St. Julia was still active, miners set off a blast one day and came to the surface to wait for the bad air to clear. To speed up the process, a man named Von Helt started a fire in an underground stove, but while he and his partner waited, both fell asleep in the warm August sunshine. Passing miners noticed smoke curling from the ground and roused the dozing men, telling them they ought to do something about their shaft that was ablaze. They quickly doused the flames but detected the presence of poisonous gasses in the mine. Despite warnings from his companion, Von Helt descended into the shaft by means of a rope tied to a burned section of ladder. When he signaled that he was out of air, his partner left to bring help. A few minutes later, as rescuers peered down the shaft, they heard the sickening impact of Von Helt's body landing on the rocks at the bottom.

Later that day, miners reached a platform 200 ft. underground and from there made several attempts to reach the corpse, but each time they were driven back by noxious fumes. Eventually, Von Helt's mangled remains were recovered and hoisted to the surface. Apparently, the unfortunate man was climbing the ladder to escape but was overcome by smoke, lost his hold and fell 300 ft.

When the news of the man's death was delivered to his sister, with whom he lived at a cabin on Iron Hill, the woman was grief-stricken. She refused to leave the cabin, eat or drink, slowly wasting away until she was carried off by the Angel of Death a few weeks later. The wandering shade that nightly made its way from Iron Hill through town to the edge of the old shaft was said to be that of the broken-hearted sister returning to the St. Julia to lament the accident that claimed the life of her only living relative.

* * * * * * *

"The mine became haunted. Strange and weird noises were heard, the calling and groaning of the spirits of the dead miners who had perished in the great explosion made the place hideous, and to work in the bowels of the earth with ghostly voices and agonized groans from departed fellow workmen sounding around one is, as any one will admit, something to try the stoutest hearts."

—Carbonate Chronicle, May 13, 1901

* * * * * * *

MAY I PICK YOUR BRAIN?

Standing isolated and forbidding near the treeless crest of the Mosquito Range, the London Mine and its environs has a singular history, ranging from mildly unusual to most unearthly. Spirits aplenty, especially those with an affinity for solitude and the scolding boreal wind, refuse to abandon the bleak landscape around the diggings.

In 1883, drillers working a stone's throw from the London in the nearby Crescent City Lode unwittingly dynamited their way into a curiosity on the 500-foot level of the mine. After the dust and powder smoke cleared, the men returned to the face of the drift to find that the blast broke through into a mineral encrusted cavern. They entered and followed it several hundred feet into the mountain. By the pale light of candles the group reportedly discovered a calcified frog, a stone axe, and in a large chamber, the petrified body of a man that fell to pieces when they attempted to pick it up. Being members of that superstitious cabal of men who probe the earth for riches, their fears got the best of them and they refused to work in the mine, returning to the surface with only tales of their discovery.

Mortality was a frequent visitor to the high basin. Some months later, in the midst of a howling dust storm on the London Extension, a railroad conductor and a pair of Swedish laborers met destruction when the train on which they were riding hit a sleeping mule and derailed. They were by no means the first or the last to join the ethereal ranks of the departed that returned to roam the desolate, rocky heights.

One uncommonly hideous murder took place in the winter of 1882, installing the soul of a covetous miner on his endless quest to procure the affection of a beautiful boardinghouse cook. John Sullivan and Henry Robinson were severely smitten with Miss Pearl the day she strolled out of the kitchen and into their hearts at the boardinghouse of the New York Mine. Isolation and difficult, dangerous work made the lure of courtship unbearable for the love-stricken men, and a rivalry developed which soon escalated into frequent dinnertime shouting matches.

During one Friday evening repast, the confrontation rose to the level of angry maledictions, with onlookers expecting a brawl to erupt at any moment. A few minutes into the conflict, the enraged Robinson jumped from his chair, ran to the corner of the room and laid hold of a pickaxe leaning against the wall. In a split second, he swung the tool high and brought it down on Sullivan's head, killing him instantly. So swift was the execution that before the other diners realized what transpired, Robinson dashed from the room and into the night, leaving his pick buried in the man's forehead.

The killer apparently made his way to Alma, disappeared, and was never brought to justice, but the confused apparition of the lovesick victim lost no time returning to possess the area around the London shaft house and the New York dining hall. Sullivan's specter generally materialized next to the kitchen stove as Pearl peeled apples for pies, and at night made its ghastly debut in the vicinity of the boardinghouse, moaning threats of revenge and trying in vain to extricate the pick from his head.

Phantoms of the Mosquito Range

"Alma had a sensation this week in the shape of a ghost, which appeared at night. People coming from the saloons about midnight saw a strange sight, or imagined they did. One night the phantom was seen near the Thomas saloon, another time it was at the bridge, on Main Street. The courageous Almaites gave chase, but when they arrived at the spot the apparition had mysteriously disappeared. Some describe it as a beautiful woman, clad in finest white lingerie. The spot where the beauty disappeared was fragrant with the perfume of roses and violets."

—*Fairplay Flume*

* * * * * * *

- Continental Chief Mine

CHAPTER THREE
SPECTRAL VICTIMS OF MURDER

As if any suburb of Leadville needed more elevation, Brooklyn Heights noses its way into the floodplain of California Gulch from the left side of the photograph. In 1880, at a cabin on the heights, a slaying was etched onto the fabric of eternity and re-enacted time and grisly time again. Spanning the gulch in this 1925 image is the trestle of the Colorado Midland Railway.
–Denver Public Library Western History Collection, X-1000634

* * * * * * *

"The murdered man's bones soon would be covered by the winter's snows and his wail wafted on frosted winds would be his only moan. In some lone spot the ghost of a murdered man would haunt the miners who would dare to intrude on the highways of Brooklyn Heights at the hour when the ghosts of dead men stalk at night."

—*Leadville Daily & Evening Chronicle, October 14, 1895*

* * * * * * *

SURREAL SIGHTS ON BROOKLYN HEIGHTS

Overlooking Leadville from its lofty perch high above the gulch, the suburb of Brooklyn Heights was laid out in eighty-four lots in 1900, but the town existed in that location since at least

1880. A glance along Harrison Ave. toward the south reveals the location of the heights, now occupied by a modern subdivision atop the ridge beyond the end of the main street.

Various ethnic groups once called the place home and a few longtime Leadville residents recall a time when numerous old homes, a stable, saloon and beer garden stood there. A pleasant grassy area surrounded by aspen and lodgepole pines provided an inviting and scenic Sunday-afternoon picnic area for women and children. Heads of households found entertainment of another sort in the bar, which featured their favorite liquid refreshment and a dancing bear.

Brooklyn Heights was connected to the gulch below by a precipitous 100-step stairway descending near the location of the long-gone GAW Brewery. Most of the structures on the heights were abandoned or demolished by 1918 and the Colorado Midland Railroad, whose grade sliced across the hillside, became extinct several years later.

During February and March of 1880, spiritual unrest plagued Brooklyn Heights, where a ghastly apparition frequented a lonely and deserted cabin. The newspaper of the day reported that a restless soul was haunting the property owned by R.H. Buck & Co. It was a forlorn rental house in which strange sights and sounds occurred both day and night. The landlord made a thorough inspection of the location and found nothing suspicious, but said it was almost impossible to keep tenants there.

"They come to me and rent the house one day, move in, and then the next day return the key, saying that the house is haunted."

Such complaints were not infrequent, and landlords of the day had an aversion to restless spirits and renters who perpetrated the "tenant with a ghost" ruse. After paying one or two months full rent, the occupants showed up several weeks later to pay the next installment, complaining that the property was haunted.

"Quaking with simulated fear, he tells a tale of horror—of a headless man seen stalking from the coal cellar, a lady in white or something invisible but groaning," said the Elbert County Banner in 1911. "Spectral visitors afford splendid subjects for gossip in the neighborhood and prospective tenants seldom fail to hear and be warned off by the story. Anxious that the report shall not get about, landlord confers with tenant, and in several such instances the result has been this—the tenant agrees to stay on, say nothing about the matter to others and to put up with the ghost, providing the rent is substantially reduced."

Apparently, this wasn't the case with the forsaken cabin on the heights. One renter in 1880 went to Buck looking for a house but was told there was only one available and that strange sounds were heard inside the place. The landlord informed the house hunters that previous tenants believed the dwelling was haunted. "The rent was almost a song and the house a fine one, and having a brave little wife, I'll take the house and live in it," one former occupant told a Leadville newsman. "I moved in that afternoon and the fun commenced."

While his wife was in town on a shopping excursion, the husband built a fire in the stove, pulled his rocking chair close to the blaze and sat down. His feet were cold, so he pulled off his boots and propped his stocking feet on the hearth. Sitting that way for some minutes he became aware of the uncomfortable sensation that he was not alone.

"I endeavored to shake off the feeling, and looking over just across the stove, saw the dim outline of a man sitting on a chair," the renter said.

His own phantom feet, resting on the stove, apparently were cold also. At first, the renter saw only the lower legs, but the rest of the form materialized as the heat oozed upward to reveal the rest of the ghostly body. The apparition looked like a Mexican and wore poor clothes, the witness said. His head was crushed in and bleeding but the injury didn't seem to bother the ghost as he basked in the warmth of the room and gazed across the stove at the new tenant.

"I was horror-stricken and powerless for a moment, and the strange eyes seemed to pierce my very soul," the occupant said. As the renter jumped from the rocker, the apparition disappeared and the man dashed from the dim interior of the cabin and into the sunshine to wait for his wife to return. Saying nothing to her about the ghost, skepticism took over. He told himself that the experience was just his imagination and that he probably dozed off as the rumors of the haunting played on his mind.

While the couple enjoyed a cup of afternoon tea, the renter looked at his wife and noticed she was staring at the stove, eyes growing larger by the moment. Once again, there sat the phantom of the late-departed homeowner, who promptly disappeared. That evening, neither husband nor wife felt like eating—their appetites replaced by thoughts of the unearthly visitor with the chilly feet and the prospect of spending the night with him as a roommate.

As the couple prepared for sleep, noises began: footsteps, the click of a revolver being cocked, a dull blow and a groan. The ghostly rattle continued for an hour, then stopped for the rest of the night.

Nothing otherworldly happened the next day until the hour to retire, when uncanny noises like those made the night before emanated from the walls, and furniture began to move across the rough wood floor. The couple covered their heads, listening from beneath the blankets as the din continued. On this night, the bed began to move, going around the room with the couple aboard before finally coming to a stop near the dressing table.

The following night, the same fantastic ordeal repeated itself, but this time the shade of the Mexican began undressing as if to join the couple in bed. No one materialized beneath the bedclothes but the following morning the wife went to a friend's house to look for lodgings where the two could stay until they procured a less spiritually active residence.

After the pair moved out, the former tenant was interviewed about his disturbing sojourn at the haunted house. He said he believed that invisible powers were at work.
"I do not want to interfere there. I shall quietly move out and leave them monarchs of the situation, free to raise merry hell just so long as they choose."

Spectral Victims of Murder

Renters during Victorian times were hesitant to live in a home in which someone was murdered in cold blood, but in 1880 Leadville, the owner of the ghost-ridden Brooklyn Heights cabin disclosed the haunting to potential tenants. How many landlords in this day and age would be so considerate?

* * * * * * *

Apparently, unknown assailants murdered and robbed the cabin's builder but were never brought to justice. After the crime, a long line of renters said they heard and saw the nightly re-enactment of the grisly deed, including the ghostly scuffle, unearthly screams and phantom gunshots.

Following its abandonment, visitors to the cabin entered and were immediately overcome with fear at the sight of a transparent figure of a man with slashed throat and bloody clothing, saying in Spanish that his comrades killed him. The apparition reportedly lingered at the scene of the murder in hopes of identifying his killers to the cabin's occupants.

"The house and lot together is not worth more than five hundred dollars. I would not give five hundred cents for it," a former renter said. "The place is haunted, or something after that nature, and I think it will have to be let alone and empty until it rots down."

Spectral Victims of Murder

News of the cabin's unholy reputation spread among the Leadville populace and soon hundreds of curious people reported seeing a ghost swaying back and forth in the window of the unoccupied structure. No one dared confront the apparition in person, even though $100 was offered to any man brave enough to enter the place.

At 8 p.m. one spring evening, seven stouthearted miners went to the newspaper office to ask if a reporter would go with them to the cabin. They were sent to Coronel McNary, owner of a cigar and tobacco stand who had the key to the haunted house. The group went to the ghost-infested homestead but returned two hours later, saying they saw the ghost and that everything previously reported was true.

"Men of iron nerve have faced the phantom, only to be palsied with horror," a Leadville daily reported. "Those to whom his ghostship has appeared, although unwilling to speak fully about the matter, decline a repetition of the visit, avowing that no money could induce them to be again subjected to the presence of the dreadfully-visaged ghoul."

On another Saturday night, 200 men gathered at a local store and went to the scene of the manifestation. What they saw was enough to send them scurrying.

"The blanched countenances and affrightened expressions of those who did go inside was sufficient to appall the rest and cause them to hurry away from the accursed place," the newspaper continued.

Stories of the unholy quarters continued to spread around town and despite popular belief that the place was haunted, a few townspeople remained skeptical and considered the rumors a clever trick for profit. Each amateur ghost hunter left a one-dollar security deposit upon checking out the key to the cabin.

"It is safe to say that two thousand people have made the unfruitful trip after the imaginary goblin, and have been thoroughly sold," said the Carbonate Weekly Chronicle. "There is not even a shade or a shadow of either ghost or haunted house, and the sell consisted in the number of miles in a dark night a crowd of curiosity seekers could be induced to walk after an apparition."

Over a two-day period, much to the disgust of the landlord, spectators fired hundreds of bullets through the window at the phantom—all from a safe distance, of course. The more the sharpshooters blasted away, the more the wispy figure in the window danced. When two gentlemen skeptics intent on collecting the cash prize finally elbowed their way through the crowd of shooters and bystanders and walked to the perforated dwelling, they threw open the door only to discover the ghost hung by the neck. They cut him down and found the specter to be merely a suit of clothes stuffed with cedar boughs and wrapped in a white sheet. It was suspended from a rafter so it would appear to float back and forth through the window of the breezy structure. The men took the spook to a local newspaper office, where it was placed on display.

Following the outbreak of ghost fever on Brooklyn Heights, dozens of Leadville residents came forward with otherworldly tales of their own.

"They have poured in from all sides in such numbers as to cause a timid person to believe that this terrestrial sphere is simply the abode of dead men and women's souls doomed," the Chronicle reporter added.

Strangely enough, in the weeks following the ghost sightings, sheet-bedecked "specters" appeared drifting in and out of dark alleys and along sidewalks on Front, Pine and State streets, scaring many Leadville residents out of their wits. Among the phantom horde was an East Seventh Street lad who read about the devilish exploits contained in _Peck's Bad Boy_ and decided to have a little fun with his father.

"The old man had come down town to get a spade sharpened or mended, or something, and the bubbling youth decided to play the ghost act on him when he returned," a Leadville daily reported. "The kid accordingly put a sheet over his head and hid in an alley, and waited for the pater familias to return. Pretty soon the old man came trudging up the walk with the spade on his shoulder. Just as he got opposite the alley the precocious boy enveloped in white sprang in front of him, and extended his white arms. Did the old man faint, or drop on his knees, or do anything else of the kind? Not much. He swung that spade in the ambient air and hit the boy a blow on the side of the head with the flat of it that knocked him clear over the fence."

Another local "spook" was a flesh and blood bartender from the Carbonate Concert Hall. His favorite victim was Edward Kennedy, a firm believer in ghosts and the resident of a house at the corner of Chestnut and Leiter streets.

Kennedy proudly told anyone who would listen how he saw and talked with the dead at his home, saying they would enter his house, stand by the bed, play on the pots and pans in the kitchen and answer questions about the spirit world. The spirits waltzed chairs around the room while the man watched with childlike fascination. Kennedy especially loved to talk to his neighbors about the midnight messengers from beyond.

For ten nights in a row it was the publican who played ghost at the Kennedy rooms. Living in the quarters directly above his victim, the barkeep perfected his routine nightly by sliding down a ladder and creeping into the sleeping man's apartment.

When the law grew weary of the ghostly pranksters' pantomimes about town, the sheriff issued an edict, saying that it probably wouldn't be considered murder if someone were to shoot a ghost. With the exception of several eighteen-carat genuine spooks, the spectral racket subsided before anyone attained ghosthood by gunfire.

****

"A practical joker at Saguache who tried to play the ghost a few days ago had three shots fired at him by the man he hoped to scare. Unfortunately none of the shots took effect."

—Stuart Chronicle, November 1, 1888

****

APPARITIONS EXPLAINED

In a brief essay that appeared in a 1905 edition of the Eagle County Blade, a psychologist detailed his skepticism of ghostly phenomena.

"Ghosts, hallucinations—pah!" he said. "I can make ghosts. You can make them. It is a mere matter of drugs and knocks on the head…We study the brain continually, and the time is now come when we can play tricks on it—when we can deluge it with ghosts, poultergorsts, djinns, hobgoblins, doppelgangers, phantoms."

Going on to say he could conjure up specific spirits by administering certain drugs, the scientist explained how to create visions of beautiful human beings.

"Suppose I want the bishop of Esk to see the phantom of a beautiful girl. I give him, then, belladonna."

To stimulate the illusion of an enchanting city with marble palaces and lovely courtyards, populated with white-robed inhabitants, the psychologist recommended a dose of opium.

Hasheesh, he added, would be the drug he would administer if he desired to drive an enemy to suicide with visions of horror.

"In hasheesh dreams, great apes strangle fair blonde women. Ruffians murder helpless old clergymen. Wild beasts, leaping on caravans, carry off in their mouths babies and little children. Cannibals hold in the depths of primeval forests orgies indescribably obscene."

Blows to specific parts of the head, he continued, could make the recipient smell phantom odors. Other well-placed whacks to the cranium would induce ghostly sounds and spectral sensations of cold.

"Therefore, don't have a superstitious belief in ghosts or hallucinations," the psychologist concluded. "For any scientist can make them to your order while you wait."

* * * * * *

"You think we are of another world. No, we have knowledge of no world but yours, though for us it holds no sunlight, no warmth, no music, no laughter, no song of birds, nor any companionship. O God, what a thing it is to be a ghost, cowering and shivering in an altered world, a prey to apprehension and despair."
—Ambrose Bierce, The Moonlit Road

* * * * * *

Spectral Victims of Murder

- Miner's Arms Saloon

When Richard Stephenson ambled into the Miner's Arms Saloon for a drink and a game of Twenty-One, little did he know he was about to be swept into the netherworld at the hand of his wife's paramour. The bullet dispatched the living being, but his immortal soul continued to pace the boardwalks along Chestnut Street.

* * * * * * *

ONE OUNCE OF LEAD

By 1877, said geologist Samuel Emmons, "The site of the present city of Leadville was an unbroken wilderness. And no suspicion of the existence of the immense basis of the district's wealth had yet entered the minds of the prospectors."

That spring, construction of a saloon on Chestnut Street became the first order of business. Another soon followed, and also a grocery, serving a population of 200 persons. Later that year, the camp was a haphazard collection of slab buildings, tents and crude shelters scattered throughout the slowly disappearing pine forest that grew near the mouth of California Gulch.

"There was no rhyme-or-reason in the town; cabins and tents were scattered everywhere among what trees were left; wagons were parked wherever they happened to stop…with people living in them and under them. Except for Chestnut and Harrison, there were no streets…only paths wandering around and through the slab-sided cabins," said Carl Akers in his description of the new camp.

Sleeping quarters weren't plentiful enough to accommodate the swelling population and empty barrels, wooden crates and piles of hay scattered along the streets and alleys provided rude shelter from the nighttime cold. Even the large coffin packing boxes piled on the sidewalk outside Rogers' undertaking establishment offered a comfortable, body-sized snoring place for one or two late comers to town. The lodging business was so lucrative that signs advertising rooms to let sprang up everywhere and saloon owners were obliged to sell floor space to new arrivals looking for temporary asylum.

"Men were glad to pay for the privilege of spreading their overcoats or blankets on the floor of a saloon and sleeping in stale smoke and the fumes of bad whiskey—an atmosphere where the oil-lamps burned with a weak and yellow flame," said Scribner's Weekly in 1879. "Perhaps the dice rattled on till morning above the sleepers' heads, the monotonous call-song of the dealers lulling them to an unquiet doze in the murky air, only to be awakened by the loud profanity of some brawler or sent cowering under the blankets to escape the too free pistol-balls that fly across the billiard-table. Even the sawdust floors of these reeking bar-rooms were not spacious enough to hold the two hundred persons a day who rushed into Leadville."

Saloon owners often found it difficult rousing the sleepers when daylight arrived in a camp where there were only two seasons: winter and the Fourth of July. To clear out the groggy men, some proprietors hit upon an effective way to do the job. Filling a large syringe with cold water and discharging the weapon into the victim's ear usually brought about the desired result, unless of course the recipient of the icy blast was already dead.

In 1879, Leadville was the liveliest town on the planet. Summertime tallies of the city's business roll showed six bakeries, four banks, 29 boarding houses, 10 boot stores, two breweries, seven construction companies, 29 groceries, 34 hotels, one hairdresser, 12 laundries, 10 liquor dealers, nine cigar and tobacco shops, 11 clothing stores, 11 liveries, 15 lodging houses, 24 real estate offices, 21 restaurants, 59 saloons, 11 sawmills, one tombstone dealer and three undertakers. Professionally speaking, 64 attorneys, 37 physicians, 23 each of notary's public, civil and mining engineers conducted business within the city limits.

By 1880, after the arrival of 15,000 more pilgrims, the city had 28 miles of streets, 13 schools with 1,100 pupils attending, five churches, 14 smelters and three hospitals that treated 3,000 patients in one year. More than 100 taprooms offered liquid refreshment and countless other resorts served up an imaginative assortment of frontier recreation. There were times when as many as 25,000 people slept within city boundaries, and at the end of February 1879 alone, 10,072 letters were mailed at the Leadville Post Office.

"Our photographers are in despair," wrote a newsman for the Leadville Eclipse in the fall of 1878. "If they take a view of our city today, it will look quite another town next week, so rapidly do new buildings go up around us.

Some 15,000 optimistic fortune seekers abided in the hills

and forests surrounding the city at a time when tearing down and stealing cabins became one of Leadville's more common nightly recreations.

"The gala night is Saturday night, when the tunnels, shafts, and levels of Fryer Hill, Carbonate Hill, and the other mining localities send down their throng of miners and 'timber men' with their wee wages in their pockets," said an 1879 edition of The New York Times. "Saloons, gambling hells, variety theatres, and dance-houses overflow, and the sidewalks are all too narrow for the crowds that stream along."

In the year 1880, Leadville was Colorado's second largest city and when the Denver & Rio Grande Railroad pulled into town from the south, the Silver City became more readily accessible from points east. Several trains a day brought wave after wave of humanity to the headwaters of the Arkansas and Leadville was the destination for anyone who wanted a crack at getting rich, have a good time or elude the law.

"Of all places on earth, this is the concentrated essence of wickedness," said an 1879 issue of The Colorado Miner detailing life in Leadville. "The most infernal cussedness exists here. Everybody is for himself and the devil seemingly for them all."

* * * * * * *

Spectral Victims of Murder

A SIDEWALK STUDY.

- "Street Scene", Scribner's Monthly
Leadville was a fascinating study in sociology during the year 1880, drawing visitors from most every corner of the civilized world...and the netherworld.

* * * * * * *

The streets and sidewalks of the city were filled with people and wagons day and night, and the educated and cultured rubbed elbows with the less genteel at every turn. Miners, gamblers, lawyers, bullies, bullwhackers, speculators, teamsters, physicians, dead beats, drifters, thieves, railroad men, engineers and smelter workers oozed along the streets and in and out of businesses. Saloons outnumbered churches five to one and had twenty times the patronage. During June of 1879, Leadville's thirsty citizenry quaffed 200 barrels of beer a day.

Leadville's devilish machinations were not hidden in some back alley but displayed openly for the world to see, much to the disgust of more straight-laced Eastern morality. Its manifold vices were the barometer by which the success of the mining camp was measured.

"The whole of Leadville and its environs was one great gaming table on which the stakes were larger and changed hands faster than in any gambling house in the world," said Colorado historian Percy Fortz in his 1941 description of life in California Gulch.

Some 1,500 seductresses employed in the local tenderloin district satiated the carnal passions of the city's mostly male populace. Among their number was a troublesome nymph named Ellen Smith, whose den stood at 123 State Street. One chilly November day, while entertaining Miss Sally Harris, a fellow courtesan of the Leadville demimonde, Ellen went into the next room to stoke the fire.

Throwing a stick of wood into the stove, she returned to the front room and sat down just as the stove exploded, blowing it to pieces, shattering light fixtures, damaging the walls and woodwork and sending a metal fragment into her visitor's hand. Apparently, a piece of dynamite, which Ellen failed to discover, was concealed in the wood, which she told police she procured from a local dealer.

Bedlam of a more felonious variety made headlines in a Sunday morning installment of the Chronicle, and gave the reader an idea of the previous night's devilry in the camp at 10,000 feet:

'HELL LET LOOSE—
THE BLOODIEST NIGHT IN LEADVILLE'S CALENDAR
* * *
MURDEROUS ASSAULT UPON A KOKOMO FREIGHTER
* * *
ASSAULT AND ROBBERY ON HARRISON AVENUE
* * *

A TENDERFOOT GARROTED ON CAPITOL HILL
* * *
DARING ROBBERY OF A MAN AT THE COMIQUE
* * *
ARREST OF A NOTORIOUS CONFIDENCE MAN'

In 1880, one eastern journalist reporting from Kokomo surmised that there were 300 men to every woman in Leadville. Census records for that year showed 14,820 people calling the city home. So plentiful were victims of disease, accidents and violence that most burials took place at night so the death toll wouldn't be so obvious. There were only 42 doctors and other assorted medicine men in Leadville, said a scribe for the Leadville Reveille, suggesting that medicos still were in short supply.

"To maintain its reputation for mortality, our city certainly needs the assistance of more doctors."

During the first years of Leadville's existence, the city was almost universally regarded as an absolute death trap. One resident told a newspaper reporter he saw 20 deaths in two days as a result of exposure and the sulfurous fumes of the reduction works. Becoming drunk and sleeping off the debauch on a floor or in the gutter usually meant a frosty death or a fatal attack of pneumonia.

Local ardent spirits weren't renowned for their purity or analgesic effects. "Drinks can be had for spots ranging from five cents to three dollars," said an 1882 edition of The Solid Muldoon. "The lower grade is composed principally of prussic acid and strychnine."

When imbibed rather than used to varnish coffins, it was responsible for the end of many a pilgrim's gilded dream, including that of an old settler named Whiskey Jack in 1878.

"He didn't fall into a prospect hole," said the Georgetown Miner, "But on last Tuesday he did lay down under a door step and went up the flume, all in his bloom, in the days of Leadville's glory."

Crime was especially bad and holdups on the avenues were an everyday and every night occurrence. Homicide left its calling card around the city regularly and most who wandered the dim streets after dark carried a pistol in hand or pocket. Despite the superabundance of firearms, the Leadville populace was noticeably well behaved.

"Nearly everyone here carries a shooter," said a visiting journalist in 1880. "And I have little doubt that to the general knowledge of this fact is due the good order and more than ordinary politeness in this place…Hence, the roughest, wickedest men are compelled to be civil and courteous, for they are uncertain who may turn loose on them."

Hundreds of saloons, concert halls and businesses of all types carried on their trade without closing their doors. Mines were producing silver by the ton and Leadville's roguishness was a tantalizing plum, ripe for the picking.

"Scarcely have the echoes of one murderous pistol shot died away when another tragedy, more horrible and infinitely more cold-blooded in its details, darkens the daily history of our camp," said a Carbonate Weekly Chronicle reporter in the wake of a September 1880 murder in downtown Leadville.

What was once the Miner's Arms Saloon stands at 132 West Chestnut, near the heart of the one-time commercial and entertainment portion of town. It was there that a former Kansas City police captain joined his ancestors at the hands of his wife's suitor just inside the door of the establishment.

Richard Stephenson, the former gendarme, and 18-year old Miss Hattie McGran, took the marriage vows in Kansas in 1879. The joy of the nuptials was short-lived, and before long the husband fell off the temperance wagon and began carousing.

"The breeze of dissipation soon ruffled the calm waters of affection," said the Leadville newsman in his 1880 description of the affair.

Stephenson made the journey from wedding bells to outright neglect over the next twelve months. He failed to clothe and feed his wife and eventually abandoned her completely. It was then that Hattie saw no future in matrimony and decided to join her widowed mother who recently moved to the Rocky Mountains and opened a boarding house at the corner of Upper Chestnut and Hemlock streets. Business was good, Susie McGran told her daughter, and Leadville had an endless supply of prospective courtiers from every walk of life.

Among her mother's boarders were Mr. Riley and a man named Thomas Morgan, the former a bartender at Delmonico's and the latter a foreman at the Leadville Gas Works. The landlady spoke highly of her daughter to both gentlemen but the stories captured Riley's interest to the point that he offered to finance the young woman's trip to the carbonate camp.

Hattie accepted without hesitation and after a week's travel, the comely Mrs. Stephenson stepped off the train and onto the dusty streets of the Cloud City. With a flawless pale complexion and jet-black hair, Hattie was one of the few extremely handsome women in Leadville, and the object of unrelenting admiration. She fell in over her head with Riley but when neighbors started to gossip about the relationship, Hattie dropped him like a bad habit and turned her flirtatious wiles toward Morgan.

Alone and seeing double in Kansas City, Stephenson received a letter from the jilted Riley saying that his wife was on the wayward path to shame. He sobered up long enough to realize Hattie was gone and lost no time following her trail to Leadville. Shortly after his arrival in camp at the end of May, he called on her but she slammed the door in his face. Stephenson, accustomed to getting his way, stayed in town and found work as a waiter at the Grand Hotel on Upper Chestnut. It was there that he began hearing breakfast-table talk of his wife and her many sweethearts.

"The story of his wife's amours was daily thrown in his teeth, and again he began a course of excessive dissipation, and frenzied by drink he would often visit the house and caused no little trouble there," the news reported of his visits to the McGran rooms.

On June 1st, Stephenson and Morgan had a row at a Chestnut Street saloon, the proprietor throwing one belligerent out the back door and sending the other packing through the front. To the patrons in attendance that night it was clear that the simmering feud was far from over.

Before long, the pair met in the hallway of the lodging house but the women convinced the hostile husband to leave before tempers flared out of control. The peace didn't last long and the four met later at a dance, the men eyeing each other menacingly.

Morgan, leaving his hat on Mrs. McGran's lap, began dancing with Hattie, while Stephenson, watching from across the room, walked over, put the hat on his head and turned to leave.

Seeing his headgear headed for the door, Morgan left Hattie in mid-step, intercepted her husband and snatched the cap from his head.

"Say your prayers, Richard Stephenson, for by heaven, you're a dead man," said Morgan as he pulled a gun from his pocket. Onlookers prevented him from using it, and Hattie, upset by the affair, went home after the two antagonists temporarily parted company. The bloodthirsty jealousy that burned inside the men left little chance that one or the other would ever see the morning. Maddened by the effects of alcohol and green-eyed jealously, Stephenson went to the Miner's Arms at midnight on September 9, where he imbibed and played cards until his adversary arrived and bought a round of drinks for the house.

Morgan stayed a short time, argued briefly with his opponent and left the tavern. Stephenson circled the room, asking the bartender and several patrons for a gun but when he was told there was none available, he walked to the end of the bar and stood a few feet from the door.

"Well, if I had a gun, by God, I'd make that fellow say Holy Mary," he was heard to say just as his rival stepped back into the saloon.

"Damn you," Morgan threatened. "I've got you now," leveling his six-shooter at the man's face.

Thinking he could disarm the gunman, Stephenson sprang forward to grab the pistol just as Morgan sent an ounce of lead whizzing through his eye and into his brain, killing him instantly. Witnesses collared the shooter, took his gun and held him for the police. Powder smoke still curled around the ceiling when officers arrived and escorted the suspect to jail. Before Stephenson's body was cold, a crowd talking of a lynching gathered outside the bar.

Spectral Victims of Murder

- Grand Hotel-1879
Upper Chestnut Street's dark alleys and dimly lit doorways enshrouded the wandering shade of Richard Stephenson as it roamed a nightly path between the Miner's Arms and the McGran boardinghouse. His former wife Hattie avoided chance encounters with her husband's ghost and stayed home at night.
–Denver Public Library Western History Collection, X-6372

* * * * * * *

Hattie and her mother stoically accepted the news of the man's death, saying he'd been looking for a fatal fuss for some time.

Even though Stephenson was tucked securely beneath the sod at the local burying ground, green envy continued to torment the dead man beyond the grave. A bullet and a coffin lid weren't enough to keep him from looking for his pretty wife, and by October his filmy shade began to materialize on Upper Chestnut Street near the foot of Carbonate Hill. It lingered in dark doorways and flickered along narrow alleys between buildings, never venturing too close to the lurid gaslight. Each evening the apparition became less transparent until by Halloween it seemed more like a living person than a ghost.

One frosty October night, two miners walking home encountered Stephenson's shade standing in the pale moonlight. The pedestrians thought it strange that despite the cold temperature, the stranger wore no coat or hat but stood with his head lowered and hands covering his face.

Inquiring if the man was sick or lost, the miners received no answer. After several attempts to find out what was wrong, the moon slipped from behind a cloud and in the eerie half-light, the man threw up his hands and raised his head, revealing an empty eye socket and the ghastly bullet hole.

"Good God, the man is dead!" one of the miners shrieked as both ran into the darkness toward their cabin on Carbonate Hill. For many years, during the months of September and October, the one-eyed phantom of Richard Stephenson continued to mortify pedestrians along Upper Chestnut. That portion of the city is now a slag-covered empty lot but the approach of Halloween still brings the vaporous, half-blind apparition of the former policeman who continues his eternal walk between the McGran Boardinghouse and the Miner's Arms Saloon in an endless search for Miss Hattie.

In the months before Stephenson's shade began walking the south end of town, the ghost of another 1880 homicide victim delivered a dire message to a local judge after she was slain in a violent encounter with her husband at their home on Capitol Hill.

* * * * * * *

"There I sees 'em warming themselves in the moonlight."
—*Newfoundland fisherman's description of ghosts,*
Creede Candle, May 14, 1921

* * * * * * *

Spectral Victims of Murder

'I'M DEAD'

Capitol Hill is a stony ridge, whose length curls around the north end of Leadville. Its summit, where it is crossed by Harrison Avenue, offers a post-card perfect view of the city's business district to the south.

Not long after the founding of Leadville, unearthly tales of spiritual unrest wafted on the air and in the conversations of hilltop residents. At that time, the area was largely a cluster of log homes and a few attractive Victorian cottages scattered among the tree stumps that bristled like a week's growth of beard on a miner's face.

"Here and there are striking exceptions to the rule of squalid cabins," said Scribner's Monthly in 1879. "On Capitol

Hill, the fashionable quarter of the camp, are several houses of imposing architecture, for they have more than four angles, have ornamental cornices, and are painted. There are a few even that have porches."

Capitol Hill's phantom ranks acquired another member on July 4, 1882 during the Independence Day celebration when Louis Kopinski, member of a local military company, was blown from atop Capitol Hill and into the next world by a faulty charge from the six-pound cannon he fired. The artillery piece, loaded with enough powder to wake the dead shattered, blowing ornamental millwork off surrounding houses and sending the young recruit to a narrow, chilly tenement at the local burial ground.

Period homes, some of the most opulent in the city still adorn the crest of the ridge as it sweeps westward and joins Ice Palace Hill, where the glorious crystal castle was built during the winter of 1896. Even today, many of these residences carry with them tales of the spectral tenants who are rumored to live there. Capitol Hill is crowned by the former Leadville High School building, now home to the National Mining Hall of Fame and Museum. Several Victorian homes, many reportedly haunted, once stood on lots now occupied by the 1960s-vintage east wing of the school.

* * * * * * *

Spectral Victims of Murder

- Capitol Hill in winter-1902

Capitol Hill has it all—quaint homes, a superb view of everything and a gentrified spirit population, whose members are content to rattle around just enough to make their presence known, even to the most skeptical Leadvillians.
Denver Public Library Western History Collection, X-6318

* * * * * * *

Mid-winter midnights at 10,000 ft. are hardly hospitable for humans, at least the ones in corporeal form. At that hour, early in 1880, the deviltry and gunshots of Lower Harrison Avenue, State and Chestnut streets were practically inaudible from Capitol Hill, where Justice Bardine slept in the bedroom of his home on West Tenth Street.

The deep winter night was otherwise peaceful until the rapping of icy fingers on wood roused the judge, who descended the stairs and opened the door to find a mysterious woman standing on the frozen porch. The pale female, Mary Rousset, lived one block away on Pittsburg Avenue. She told him to get up.

"I'm dead," she informed the magistrate.

Bardine was more irritated than surprised by the strange visitor. Many years of dispensing justice from the bench had accustomed him to the oddities of human nature. However, the appearance of the ashen woman at the witching hour and her terse pronouncement aroused his curiosity.

Inquiring as to her identity, the justice asked how long she'd been dead and who her murderer was. Mary responded, identifying herself and saying that her husband took her life at their cabin a short time earlier. In fact, he was there right now killing the children, she told the judge, asking him to go immediately and stop the murders. Bardine had no intention of going out but said he would call a police officer to investigate and if necessary, have the enraged man taken to jail.

"Oh, no you won't! You lock up my old man, Judge, and I'll tear out your dirty old eyes. You send an officer after my old man if you dare," threatened the apparition before it flitted away from the door and into the night.

Despite the lateness of the hour, thoughts of the curious visitor haunted Bardine. Thinking that her children might be in harm's way, the justice pulled on his clothes, locked the door to his house and wove a skeptical path through the snow to the Rousset cabin.

Approaching the front door of the couple's home, the lurid light of the lamp the judge carried revealed the freshly dead corpse of a woman. There, clad in torn and bloodstained clothes, Bardine discovered the lifeless body of Mary, whose head and face were covered with the mortal wounds she received during the death struggle.

What became of the children or the murder was lost in history, but the pioneering spirit of Mary Rousset succeeded in making the final journey from Pittsburg Avenue to Tenth Street to reveal the identity of her killer to the only man who could bring him to justice.

* * * * * * *

"A cow wandered into a Leadville residence the other night and fell through the floor into the cellar. The family who were all in bed believed the noise to be caused by ghosts and nearly died of fright before the daylight brought them courage to investigate."

—Buena Vista Democrat, February 25, 1891

* * * * * * *

Spectral Victims of Murder

MIND VS. MATTER

"When you think you see a ghost, how can you tell whether it really is a ghost or not?" was the question posed to readers in the Summit County Journal in 1903.

In order to determine if the apparition was real or a product of the viewer's mind, a writer offered a simple scientific test to be performed when confronted by a ghost.

While looking at the manifestation with both eyes, the news article recommended, the seer places a finger on the outside of the upper eyelid and gently depresses one eyeball. If the phantom is real, two images of the ghost will be seen. If it is a figment of the mind, there will be only one image. This method can be tested using any object within the field of vision.

The advice was given, the newspaper said "…because of the many nervous and brain-wearied people who see spooks, and to whom it would be better that they should know that the trouble is within themselves, and so seek a capable doctor, than to continue to be haunted, as they believe, by the supernatural."

* * * * * * *

"For a moment the Canterville ghost stood quite motionless in natural indignation; then, dashing the bottle violently upon the polished floor, he fled down the corridor uttering hollow groans, and emitting a ghastly green light. Just, however, as he reached the top of the great oak staircase, a door was flung open, two little white-robed figures appeared, and a large pillow whizzed past his head! There was evidently no time to be lost, so, hastily adopting the Fourth Dimension of Space as a means of escape, he vanished through the wainscoting, and the house became quite quiet."

— Oscar Wilde, The Canterville Ghost

Dangerous Apparitions

"Every once in a while a ghost crops up in the columns of the daily or weekly press. This ghastly spirit sometimes assumes the part of a promenader on some lonely road, who petrifies belated travelers out of their wits. Few persons credit these blood curdling accounts of the doings of his ghostship. But there is a tenement which is unquestionably haunted at times. When a nervous malady attacks the human tenement, the manifestation is most appalling, and usually most violent at night. Sleeplessness, if nervousness is disregarded, becomes chronic, and the entire system suffers in consequence. For disturbance of the nerves, Hostetter's Stomach Bitters is a thorough remedy, as it also is for malaria, rheumatism, dyspepsia, constipation and biliousness."

--Leadville Daily & Evening Chronicle, June 20, 1898

Spectral Victims of Murder

No one is alive today to testify whether or not Dr. Hostetter's elixer was effective in banishing ghostly apparitions, but the abundance of the doctor's empty bottles found in trash middens throughout the West speaks to the popularity of the remedy.

Spectral Victims of Murder

RATHWAY'S SPECTER

Leadville residents were beside themselves during the summer of 1887 when they heard reports that the ghost of a girl who was murdered in March was seen several times during one week in the months following her death. Those unfortunate enough to encounter the degraded spirit said she appeared near the spot where she was killed in the alley behind the 400-block of Harrison.

Leadville businessman Jonas Bidder and his trusted steed didn't need the eyeball test to know exactly what they saw in their mid-summer encounter with the spirit of Carrie Rathway in downtown Leadville. Bidder, a resident of the avenue, met the young woman's specter while driving along the avenue at 12 a.m. At the corner of West Fifth and Harrison, Bidder's horse sensed something it didn't like, stopped suddenly, snorted with fear and began trembling where it stood. Seeing nothing, the rider tried to reassure the animal but it bolted to one side and threw him to the ground. Bidder cursed, stood up, dusted himself off and glanced in the direction of the alley where the murder took place. There he saw the specter of the dead woman wearing a white robe and pointing to the spot where her body was found. On her face was an expression of reproach, and as the man watched in amazement the apparition vanished from sight.

Bidder was forced to walk the remainder of the distance to his home, his horse having run away. He found the animal behind a load of hay inside his barn on Front Street.

Five years later, two pedestrians who encountered Rathway's ghost at the same spot were foolish enough to follow her into the forlorn and haunted alleyway.

★ ★ ★ ★ ★ ★ ★

"It is widely believed in Maryland that a horse has the power of seeing ghosts."
　　　　　　　　　　　—Telluride Daily Journal, January 28, 1902

★ ★ ★ ★ ★ ★ ★

Spectral Victims of Murder

What was once Tompkins Hardware still stands at the corner of West Fifth and Harrison Avenue. Around 1890, numerous sightings of the same phantom occurred in the alley behind this building

SLAIN BEHIND THE SADDLE ROCK

In the summer of 1892, six nights after ghosts were seen at the Midland Depot, Miss Rathway's lost soul, trapped in the labyrinth between Leadville and the next world, materialized again in the downtown area. Because of the number and frequency of ghost sightings during that year, a reporter from a local newspaper speculated that Leadville was a clearinghouse for spirits of the dead.

At 11:30 p.m., Dan Bowden, an employee at the Hotel Kitchen, and his friend George DeFrance stood at the corner of Fifth and Harrison in front of Tompkins Hardware talking with friends. The pair decided to take a walk and get some fresh air before going home. Strolling west toward Pine Street, they stepped into the alley behind Harrison, and looking south to the rear of the Saddle Rock Restaurant, saw the apparition of a woman at the head of the desolate backstreet leading east from

Pine. The specter, with long dark hair and a flowing white robe, looked vaguely familiar to Dan as it turned and drifted slowly down the alley toward the west.

Dan and George followed close behind her for one-half block, when the spirit stopped, turned and beckoned to one of the men to go to her. Dan, the chosen one, let out a yell and with his friend close at his heels, dashed to the nearest house. Finding the door locked, Dan threw his weight against it and broke it in. Once inside, they collapsed breathless on the floor while the terrified occupants of the shanty, in bed at the time, took refuge under the blankets and lay motionless, terror-stricken at the sudden intrusion. They later threatened to have the two men arrested for breaking into their home.

Regaining their senses, Bowden and DeFrance returned to the alley to investigate further, but the spirit was gone. Dan said he recognized the apparition as Carrie Rathway, who died some years earlier after a love affair went awry.

* * * * * * *

"It was a fearful night, the wind sobbed and wailed round the house like lost spirits mounting their doom; the rain beat upon the casements, and the trees, writhing in torture of the fierce blast, groaned and swayed until their tops almost swept the earth.
It was just such a night that Nancy Black died. What a fearful night for the soul to leave its earthly home and go out into the vast, unknown future."

—*Castle Rock Journal*, January 7, 1898

* * * * * * *

GOLD, GREED AND THE GALLOWS

Stepping to the front of the executioner's platform erected on the brow of a hill not far from the foot of West Fourth Street, convicted murderer Si Minich prophesied to a crowd of thousands of Leadvillites gathered at his feet.

"Some of you here today will meet me again, and some of you will not, because you will not be able to go where I go to," he told the onlookers who awaited his hanging. "I am an innocent man. Good-by to all! Good-by!"

In unison, the throng bade farewell to the condemned as he dutifully stepped back to his place beneath the hangman's noose that waved above his head in the winter breeze. Within the hour,

Minich's soul was dispatched out of Leadville and his body set sail for the Evergreen shore.

Minich paid the ultimate price for the murder of Sam Baldwin. Two years earlier, on Oct. 13, 1884, Baldwin, a teamster employed at the Daisy Mine, boarded his rig and drove two miles to a grove of trees in Evans Gulch to harvest timbers. When suppertime came and went and the woodcutter still hadn't returned, his companions at the mine mounted a search. Finding his mules and unattended wagon, they scoured the ground along the edge of the trees, finding Baldwin's hat lying among the frostbitten remnants of the alpine vegetation. Nearby was sprawled the body of the unfortunate man, dead of a gunshot wound to the head.

None of Baldwin's companions were surprised to discover that he was waylaid and robbed of the $1,200 in twenty-dollar gold pieces he was known to carry sewn into the lining of his coat. Nearby, searchers found a cloth hood with holes cut out for the eyes. Detectives searched a nearby cabin where they found pieces of the same black cloth from which the hood was fashioned. The cabin's occupants, including Minich, were arrested.

After the murder, evidence cleared all suspects except Minich, who was penniless until the day of Baldwin's death. That afternoon, he crossed Mosquito Pass, opened an account and deposited $360 in gold in an Alma bank. Detectives followed his trail over the pass and brought him back to Leadville to stand trial. It was likely Minich would have tasted justice that night at the hands of the angry crowd milling outside the jail, had the sheriff not fortified the lockup with extra guards.

In the days and weeks following the homicide, the Baldwin tale took a supernatural turn. A pair of men digging holes in a vacant lot aroused suspicion. When asked about their activities, they said a local fortune teller directed them to the place, telling them that there they could find the stash of missing gold coins. In Evans Gulch, miners who passed the murder scene on their way to and from work said the stand of timber where he died was haunted. The sight of the bloodstained ground and the memory of Baldwin's mutilated body obliged passersby to give the unhallowed place a wide berth along the trail to the Daisy Lode.

Spectral Victims of Murder

Sam Baldwin was murdered and robbed among the weathered tree stumps in this old timber-cutting area located in Upper Evans Gulch. The grisly deed set in motion a series of peculiar events that would affect Leadville for more than a decade.

* * * * * * *

One tunneler, returning to Leadville after a day's labor at the mine, warily made his way past the cursed spot as evening began to darken the grove of trees. Above the steady plodding of his horse's hoofs, he heard the sound of a heavy blow and a disembodied cry for help followed by the report of a pistol. The miner's horse, trembling, sensed something it didn't like, stopped in its tracks and refused to pass the spot where the grisly deed took place. Pistol in hand, the rider dropped to the ground and peered toward the trees amid the sound of murmuring voices, moans and a phantom shout. Hearing a footfall behind him, he turned, but found he was alone. Peering nervously into the trees, the terrified traveler saw the figure of a hatless, coatless man emerge, face covered in blood, staggering down the slope toward the spot where Baldwin's body was discovered. The figure fell twice, each time getting up and continuing its fatal march before finally fading from sight. The horror-stricken miner ran from the scene, only to discover that his horse had disappeared.

He found the animal patiently waiting two miles downstream in the settlement of Evansville.

Minich's trial began in January 1885, and physical evidence as well as the suspect's conflicting stories led to his March conviction and sentencing. After an unsuccessful appeal to the state supreme court, the judge set an execution date of Feb. 5, 1886. A new gallows was constructed for the ceremony to be held on the west side of Leadville, not far from where the Boulevard Road crossed the hill above City Cemetery.

Fascinated at the prospect of a public hanging, crowds of Leadville residents milled around the courthouse in the days leading up to the execution, hoping for a chance to gaze upon the countenance of the doomed man. Sheriff Lamping admitted groups of curious visitors, who passed Minich's cage single file, some stopping briefly to speak with the felon while others hurried out when greeted by his stony stare. The parade only served to unravel the prisoner's nerves and the sheriff denied admission to any more spectators.

That night, Minich asked for a tete-a-tete with Ellen Smith, a daughter of the Leadville half-world who also was serving time in the county jail. Lamping denied the appeal and instead presented Minich with a new suit of clothes to wear to the gallows.

Languishing in jail on the eve of his hanging, a single candle illuminated the cell, casting stark shadows on the walls, floor and ceiling.

"I am going to God with a clear conscience," the doomed man told a reporter. "And when the people hang me today, I will be a lamb led to the slaughter, the victim of perjury, malice and conspiracy—I am innocent of the murder of Sam Baldwin."

Cigars, apples, oranges, candy and oysters and an hourly sip of whiskey were a few of the delicacies he enjoyed during his last long, mostly sleepless night. On the morning of execution day, Minich confessed to being one of a pair of men who murdered Baldwin during the attempt to steal his gold. He said that he and three other men hatched the plan, fashioned the hoods and later divided up the gold at the Ruby Saloon on State Street. Mattie Lee, former mistress of the Ruby's proprietor, later gave police the names of the accomplices, including that of her ex-paramour.

Judgement Day for Minich was bright and cold as he climbed the scaffold.

"There was not a cloud in the sky," said a writer for the Silver Standard. "The doomed man gazed about upon the motley throng and then let his eyes wander to the snow-capped mountains round about him. His last look upon the beautiful scene was a long and earnest one."

After shaking hands with everyone on the platform and pulling on a new pair of shoes made especially for the occasion, Minich was jerked from the gallows and into the next life at 17 minutes until 2 p.m. His leave of absence lasted one week, and the malefactor's restless spirit rose from the dead to put in an appearance at the city lockup.

"The prisoners in the county jail are much excited over the alleged visit from the ghost of their late companion and fellow citizen, Si Minich," the newspaper said on February 13.

On that day, a woman the newspaper referred to as an "ancient shrew", a State-Street inhabitant named Mrs. Floody, was picked up for disturbing the peace and deposited in the cell occupied several days earlier by Minich. She and Smith, her ever-popular erring sister, quickly struck up a lively conversation.

"The new arrival had taken enough on board to stimulate her colloquial powers, and was murdering the Queen's English, when suddenly she faltered and ridding herself of a fiendish yell, tried to point out to Ellen the ghost of Minich," the newspaper reported.

Ellen, who shed a few tears of her own for the doomed man when he was led from the cell to the gallows, told the terror-crazed Mrs. Floody to keep quiet or she would scare the specter away from where it stood. The other prisoners, awakened from sleep by the racket, stretched their necks and peered through the bars to catch a glimpse of the returned spirit of the executed man.

Meanwhile, at a local undertaking establishment, Minich's tenantless corpse lay mortifying on the embalming table pending burial instructions from friends or relatives. Since no one claimed the body and famished members of the town's canine population were beginning to scratch at the mortician's door, the deceased was committed to the potter's field at Evergreen Cemetery.

In the years following the execution, the condemned man's final words would come true and many Leadville residents were destined to come face to face with the convicted murderer once again in a series of events shrouded in mystery.

"Incantations, charms, hoodoos and anti-hoodoos were flying thick and fast on several blocks on the east side," said a newspaper of the day. "If the average wayfarer, who might be skeptical on these points were to venture out late at night in certain quarters, he might run afoul of some sort of witch charm that might have some sort of effect on his nerves."

Speculation on matters of the occult swelled following a series of strange deeds carried out by a local priestess of the Black Arts named Kate Rothenberg. She apparently placed a hex on a man who went to her for mediumistic advice. The consultation went sour and he slapped her after she told him never to darken her doorstep again. Indeed, the man succumbed, becoming sick and deranged. In order to break her spell, he was told by another occultist, he would have to draw blood from the nose or mouth of the woman who bewitched him. He promptly found Kate on the street, slapped her again and bloodied her nose. By the time he was hauled into court on assault charges, he was well on his way to recovery.

Justice Parker heard the case but was faced with the dilemma of locating certain witnesses, including Si Minich.

"There are several spooks and such creatures brought into the case, and it looks to be impossible to get at the facts without some of them here," said the judge. "Si Minich ought surely to be here. My constable is perfectly willing to serve the papers, but the difficulty will be to find Si."

Some suggested that if the officer did try to seek out the wraith of the departed man, he would need to don an asbestos suit because Minich was undoubtedly hurled into Pluto's hottest furnaces following the hanging.

By 1898, as the remains of Si Minich decayed under the pines at Evergreen, local sorcerers recognized the opportunities

Spectral Victims of Murder

an executed murderer could bestow upon them. In their effort to influence and bewitch Leadville residents for personal gain, practitioners of the dark arts began invoking magical powers they believed the murderer could provide.

"Just outside that portion of the cemetery devoted to the interment of those people who have died an honest death, there lies a lonely grave," said the newspaper scribe. "On a piece of plain board, worn by wind and weather, though yet legible, can be traced the name 'Si Minnick', who in the early days, met death at the hands of the hangman to expiate the crime of murder."

Spectral Victims of Murder

- Grave of Si Minich
What horrors lay beneath the decay of pine needles that carpet the sunken burial vault containing the skeletal relics of Si Minich? It's nothing frightening—just a neat pile of bones and a dreadful grimace.

* * * * * * *

  Meanwhile, other practitioners of voodoo were casting their charms in the neighborhoods along the lower slopes of Little Strayhorse Ridge. Rothenberg and her next-door neighbor awoke one morning to find piles of dirt on their doorsteps. Dozens of other east-side residents also discovered smallish piles of earth deposited on their porches by enemies who hoped to visit evil on them. A simple sweeping would do no good, since most were well aware of the dreadful power of dust taken from the grave of Si Minich. As a result, the mound of dirt over his bones, originally consisting of enough clay to bewitch the entire city of Leadville, gradually began to disappear.

> *"Home and fireside naught will save,*
> *When cursed thrice from murderer's grave.*
> *Dirt that covers hangman's prey,*
> *Bringeth misery should it lay*
> *By hearth, by home, by yard, by door,*
> *Thrown thrice in the midnight hour."*

This baleful prophecy, quoted by a Leadville woman who professed some knowledge of such ancient incantations, came one night in an east-side council meeting to discuss strategies to rid the neighborhood of one old woman's devilish deeds. It was common knowledge that the conjuror was in consort with the ghost of Si Minich and was dabbling in the Black Arts while her neighbors slept.

"This female is at work in her kitchen boiling strange compounds, in which cats' hearts, mouse eyes, toad's livers and deadly weeds gathered in the full of the moon are a few of the milder ingredients," the press reported. "Such cabalistic practices, of course, did not tend to make the ancient dame very well liked in the neighborhood."

One evening, bucket in hand, the priestess shrouded herself in black and made her way through the burying ground to the mound of earth covering the remains of the murderer. She filled the pail with dirt from the grave and returned to her house. At the witching hour of midnight, she emerged carrying the bucket, and going house to house, tossed hexed handfuls of dust at the door of each neighbor against whom she held a grudge. With every throw, she uttered the spell necessary to activate the charm. Neighbors, finding their porches soiled the next morning, set out to catch the witch in the act. That night, their suspicions were verified when they witnessed the malevolent ritual. On the third night, the neighborhood women were determined to break the spell before the third and final phase was carried out. When the sorceress again emerged at midnight, the victims chased her back into her home with a shower of rocks. The witch fired back, heaving handfuls of clay and curses at her tormenters. The show of force was enough to put an end to the hex and bring an uneasy peace to the east side of town.

For a brief interlude during the 1880s, Si Minich gleamed across Leadville like some brilliant meteor and was lost in the outer darkness. Since then, the passage of time has obliterated the superstitions that once held the minds of many Leadville residents captive. But hidden deep in the pauper's section of Evergreen Cemetery, where the somber, dense forest blocks out all but the most potent rays of the mid-summer sun, the life force slowly ebbs from the bones of the convicted murderer who rests beneath a remarkably thin layer of earth.

* * * * * * *

"The altitude of the Carbonate Camp would seem to favor the coming of spiritual friends, for whether they consider the flight of a few thousand feet of any moment or not, it is nevertheless an indisputable fact that they swoop down among us from the airy realms above oftener than upon towns and cities situated in the foot-hills and valleys of the Centennial state."

—*Leadville Daily Herald, January 16, 1886*

* * * * * * *

'YOU THOUGHT I WAS DEAD'

Some days after being dispatched out of Leadville by a slug from a .38 caliber Smith & Wesson in the hands of Lang, the tonsor, the shade of a murdered East Sixth Street cobbler returned to earth to visit his neighbor as he played Twenty-One at Hyman's Saloon in 1886.

Fredrick Stisser was a German, a card-writer by trade, who earned a meager living by penning postal cards and letters for unschooled Leadville residents. One Monday evening, curiosity drew him off the street and into the popular gambling resort to court Lady Luck at cards. Stepping up to the table, he gleefully threw down a single nickel and prepared to draw from the deck. Bored by the monotony of the game, the experienced players laughed fit to burst at Stisser's innocent optimism and meager wager. Noticing their enjoyment, the German gave in to the spirit of recklessness and played two nickels instead of one. He drew cards totaling twenty-five.

Dejected at the loss and debating whether to bet again, Stisser was suddenly startled by a cold, clammy hand placed on his shoulder and the sound of a hollow voice saying, "Fred, you thought I was dead, didn't you? Well, you see I am not."

Spinning around to look at the speaker, Mr. Stisser toppled out of his chair and fell to the floor in shock, aghast at the sight of his dead friend Sam, the cobbler. The pallid visitor gave a ghostly smile, turned on his heel and said, "Well, Fred, I'll see you again." as he ambled toward the bar room at the front of the building.

Recovering from the shock and hoisting himself off of the floor, Stisser quickly followed the specter into the saloon, and seeing no one but the bartender, asked him if he believed in ghosts.

"Not until now," was the barkeep's reply. "That person who has just passed out of the door is undoubtedly the ghost of Sam Peabody, the murdered shoemaker."

MURDERED IN ROOM 13

"This is Mary Coffey and I'll be checking out at 7 o'clock," said the woman who called the desk clerk at 2 a.m. from the room on the second floor of the Delaware Hotel in early June of 2011.

It was a routine request for the night attendant. Promising to make the necessary arrangements, he thanked the caller and hung up the receiver. However, the otherwise uneventful evening at the front desk took an eerie twist when the clerk, unable to locate anyone by the name of Coffey in the hotel registry realized that Room 2, where the call originated, was vacant.

Reporting the events of the evening to a supervisor at the conclusion of the night shift, the clerk was stunned to learn that Mary Coffey, who was mortally wounded and died at the hotel 122 years earlier, would not be checking out anytime soon.

Born in Boston, Mary Gallagher took the wedding vows with her fiancé, Jerry Coffey, in 1879 at Eureka, Nevada. The couple had six children, four of whom died as the couple followed the whims of mining from camp to camp throughout the West. In 1888, the Coffeys left Butte, Montana to seek their fortune in Leadville, but the children's deaths, an errant lifestyle and Mr. Coffey's green-eyed jealousy left the marriage on unstable ground. The family found lodging at the Delaware in the fall of 1889, and while residing in Leadville, trouble was no stranger at the couple's door. Earlier that year, Jerry Coffey began to show signs of insanity when he threatened to kill his wife with a miner's candlestick and then went on to rip her clothing to shreds. He also had his wife arrested on charges of adultery, which were eventually dropped. Three months later, she had him locked up for assault after he took two shots at the police officer who went to their home to serve a warrant.

Mr. and Mrs. Coffey and their daughters Mary and Maggie lived in Room 13 at the Delaware for two weeks prior to the murder that sent the 27-year old mother's restless ghost on its endless wanderings among the rooms and corridors of Leadville's vintage hotel.

On November 4, as she lay paralyzed and dying from a pair of gunshot wounds received a few hours earlier at the hand of her husband, Mary told Judge Lynch her version of what happened. Her story was verified by witnesses. The previous evening, she said, a sick friend down the hall named Mrs. Robinson, asked Mary to sit with her. This she did, playing cards and talking until returning to her room at 11 p.m. Early the next morning, Mary went back to the ailing friend's room to check on her condition. Jerry Coffey, suspecting that his wife was being unfaithful, was on the bed waiting for her when she arrived home.

"Where were you?" the enraged husband demanded, accusing her of drinking, leaving the children alone and spending the night with another man.

Receiving no response, Mr. Coffey jumped up and grabbed his wife by the throat.

"I'll fix you," he yelled, pulling a .41-caliber pistol from his coat pocket, adding that he'd intended to kill her for a long time. Mary slipped out of his grasp and ran to the door but was felled by a bullet from her husband's revolver. Seated on the floor near the foot of the bed, her blue calico dress bathed in blood, the woman was prostrated by another shot to the back. Calmly dropping the gun in the water closet, the shooter jerked his boots on, stepped over his wife and passed through the door into the hallway. The sound of shots and screams attracted the attention of other hotel guests, who leaned out of their apartments to see Jerry Coffey striding toward the stairs. They summoned police. Once outside the hotel, Coffey ran up Seventh Street and officers took him into custody by the time he reached Poplar.

"The only reason that I can give for his action is that he was crazy from jealousy," the wounded wife told the sheriff later that day.

"She harassed the life out of me," was Mr. Coffey's cold justification for the assault when asked by a reporter why he shot his wife.

Mary Coffey died peacefully two days later on November 6, 1889, but the violence surrounding her demise and the emotion of leaving two daughters alone compelled the woman's soul to remain at the corner of Seventh and Harrison. After more than 100 years, Mary's shade lives on at the hotel, caught between heaven and Leadville, tenderly looking after sick guests and tucking children into their beds at night.

CHAPTER FOUR
GHOSTS IN THE GRAVEYARD, ETC.

> "The idea of groping among tombstones and communing with ghosts and goblins for a livelihood causes a cold chill to run down my back. No, gentlemen, I must refuse."
>
> -- *Las Animas Leader, May 28, 1875, after L.W. Cutler was offered a job as Las Animas City Sexton*

REQUIESCAT IN PACE

City Cemetery, Leadville's "dreary city of the carbonate dead", occupies several acres of rocky ground near the west end of Elm Street. The former graveyard, now indistinguishable, is beneath and around the area occupied by the Lake County High School football field. Early records indicated that at least 251 official burials took place here from 1877 until 1879 when land was acquired for Evergreen Cemetery, one mile to the north. Then, as it is today, the city's burial ground was an austere, unremarkable place. It never had more than two or three marble headstones scattered among dozens of pieces of plain board with names and dates marked in pencil or lamp black.

"There were no flowery lawns, sparkling fountains, shady nooks, grassy plots nor artistically carved marble," said the Daily Chronicle in May 1879. "The weeping willow, the wandering walks, the turning arbor, the rustic chair—there were none of these. In short, there is nothing about the burying place for the dead of Leadville to make a well man desire to die."

By 1882, said a Leadville daily, almost every indication that the place was a cemetery was obliterated by both man and beast. "Gross weeds wave over the sepulchers of the sleepers. The emblems of poor Yorick are strewn hither and thither by some invasion of cattle, hogs or horses."

The D&RG railroad grade also passed over a portion of the graveyard, making peaceful sleep impossible for the dead, especially when the lament of some shrill engine whistle sent the herds scampering over the mounds, leveling them and uprooting the primitive headboards.

Markers that weren't destroyed by animals or the high-country elements met with destruction of another sort.

"There were men who used them for kindling wood," said the original cemetery sexton. "You wouldn't think it, but there's many a pan of bacon been cooked over the blazes of head boards that were stolen from that place."

In the early 1880s, City Cemetery tenants who could be located were scooped out and moved to Evergreen, but scores of corpses still repose in the banks of California Gulch, long forgotten in the gold-bearing gravels of the gully.

"I'm afraid that in years to come," said the undertaker two years later, "when all indications of a graveyard are gone, that if a prospector should happen to pitch his tool there, he'll find bones before he exposes carbonates."

More than a few souls of those incumbent townsfolk, ushered unknown and unlamented into the presence of the Almighty, still ply the Leadville diggings in spirit form. One such specter made life miserable for nearby neighbors several years later.

"A ghost of the good, old-fashioned sort, with the necessary number of groans, chains and all that helps make a ghost delightful, has been appearing in the vicinity of the old Elm Street cemetery," said an edition of the Leadville Daily & Evening Chronicle about a series of unearthly events that shuddered through the neighborhood in 1887.

During the fall of the year, when most of the silver city's astral inhabitants tended to come calling, odd events began to occur at the derelict burying ground. Residents living in nearby homes noticed a vaporous human form ooze out of the earth every evening at 9 p.m. The spirit's appearance caused no end to agitation among the Austrians on the lower-west side. Nightly, with the exception of the Sabbath, said a resident of Stringtown Avenue, the spirit rose from the grave, and uttering a disembodied groan, kicked over the wooden marker and began to walk the earth. At times, it carried a lantern in its hand.

Ghosts in the Graveyard, Etc.

When the ghost frenzy of the 1880s was at full tilt, it took a very clever baking powder salesman to lay the City Cemetery phantom to rest.

✶ ✶ ✶ ✶ ✶ ✶

Following the path of eternal repetition, the phantom strode from the grave to the railroad freight cars that stood on the nearby siding. Climbing aboard a car, the ghost delivered an oration in Greek or Latin—none of the locals were quite sure which. At the conclusion of the speech, the silver-tongued spook climbed down and took up a position where the wagon road crossed the nearby railroad tracks. There he waited in semi-transparency for unsuspecting travelers to pass.

When unwary pedestrians reached the crossing, the spirit groaned menacingly, "Money or your life!" Terrified victims usually gave up their wallets when confronted by the ghost. Surrendered money pouches fell through the phantom hand and onto the ground, where they would be found the next morning by the first fortunate pilgrim to pass the haunted spot.

After the terrified victim turned tail and scurried away toward the lights of Leadville, the ghost made his way back to its resting place, and standing up the old marker, disappeared into the earth. The routine continued for many weeks, until residents held a Sunday-night meeting to decide how to put an end to the spirit's nocturnal plunders.

Ghosts in the Graveyard, Etc.

Believing the ghost to be the soul of an old highwayman, one resident suggested getting a Concord coach and driving it by the cemetery at 9:30 p.m. If the ghost showed up to relieve the passengers of their money, the committee members would jump out, catch the shadowy thief in the act and put an end to the charade. The conspirators decided against the plan because of the high cost of hiring the coach. The alternative called for the vigilantes armed with sticks and rocks to wait for the apparition behind the freight car. Several miners in the group favored the idea of a spirited thrashing and opted for the latter of the two schemes.

At 9 p.m. on the appointed night, the phantasm stepped from the grave, pronounced his edicts on the car and was met with a volley of rocks and sticks. The ghost was uninjured—rocks flew through the body and sticks fell on empty space. One miner fired two bullets through the misty form, but to no effect. Instead, the specter got his Irish up and threatened the attackers, who by now were convinced that the apparition was real and made a hasty retreat.

Round one went to the ghost, but fortune favored the neighbors in the encounter that followed.

The day before the showdown at the graveyard, there arrived in Leadville a baking powder salesman who heard about the nightly apparition and set out to investigate. Telling his friends he had a proven method for laying ghosts to rest, the seller went to the cemetery at sundown, concealed himself at the freight car and waited. Promptly at 9, the spirit stepped from the tomb, stood on the car and gave his oratory while the salesman listened attentively.

"That's very interesting," he told the phantom at the conclusion of the discourse. "Don't you ever get tired of hearing it?"

When the ghost replied in the affirmative, the solicitor gave a political speech of his own.

"Don't you have anything more interesting?" the spirit inquired, to which the traveling salesman said "no", but that he would continue by telling a story.

One time in the Canadian woods, the peddler said, he was

walking with his sample case when he saw a bear approaching him. The itinerant vendor abandoned the grip and scooted up the nearest tree. Growling savagely, the bruin was about to ascend in pursuit of the offensive human when he took an interest in the powder case. The animal ripped it open and ate a container of baking powder. Captivated by the taste of the product, the bear devoured another ten cans of the stuff.

Because it is such good baking powder, the salesman told the ghost, the bear's head began to swell until it finally exploded.
"I regard it as ample proof that the baking powder I sell is the best on the market—but must you go?" he asked the phantom, who already was headed for the grave.

The spirit replied, "I will trouble these people no more. In my time, I was considered a very good liar, but I could never cope with you, so that if you remain in this country, I must depart. If you came here with the intention of driving me away, you have succeeded in your purpose; adieu!"

With these words, the ghost climbed into the grave for the last time, pulled in the tombstone after him, and tranquility once again descended over the forsaken burying ground.

Ghosts in the Graveyard, Etc.

"Now it is the time of night
That the graves, all gaping wide,
Every one lets forth his sprite—
In the church-way paths to glide."

—William Shakespeare, *A Midsummer Night's Dream*

'CAN'T AN OLD LADY CELEBRATE?'

Following a little careful scrutiny, what appeared to be ghosts at first glance weren't always genuine spooks. Unexplained lights, queer sounds and common coincidences sometimes created as much terror as the appearance of a bona fide phantom. During a spiritualistic age in a city populated with mostly common folk, many of which brought their own folktales from Europe, there existed a healthy respect for ghostly manifestations. Practical jokers heightened the public's otherworldly awareness by regularly summoning spirits of the departed with cleverly laid capers, such as the one hatched by some west-side wags in 1884.

"A sensation was started at West end, (13th ward) Sunday morning by a report that a German named Jensen had committed suicide by throwing himself head first down a thirty foot well," said the local news. "After a crowd of some hundred or more men, women and children and reporters had gathered about the water shaft Jensen appeared in their midst and began to laugh. It was all an idle Sunday morning sell."

Evergreen Cemetery was the sight of another curious, but explainable event at the turn of the 20th Century. One winter midnight in 1900, the residents of Capitol Hill were startled by the sight of luminous shapes gathered at a grave in Evergreen Cemetery. Night after night, the spirits hovered and danced among the dark branches of the trees as the neighbors peered from the back doors of their homes perched on the hill a couple of hundred yards distant.

In an effort to unravel the mystery, a ghost debunker and a local reporter decided to brave a nighttime visit to the burying ground. As they descended from the safety of their vantage point atop Capitol Hill, they counted five indistinct forms floating above the graves at equal distances from each other. The investigators, particularly the scribe, approached the phantom gathering cautiously.

"With his hands on his charms, he proceeded slowly, seeing hosts of dark shadows that looked like disembodied spirits, crouching behind monuments and pine trees, while elves, spooks and witches seemed to take form in the trees," the newspaper said." The forms appeared to sway to and fro from among the trees. A groaning sound was heard."

Approaching the cemetery, the pair discovered that the ghostly lights emanated from the windows of a two-story house. The bottom floor was dark and the light of candle flames sputtered in each of the five upper windows. Curtains hanging above the tallows gave them a pale, phantom-like appearance. Approaching the house, the men found the door locked and with little hesitation they left the graveyard with the mystery only partly solved.

- Evergreen entrance and old G.A.R. Hospital-1907
With the exception of the gate, the advertisement and the old Grand Army of the Republic Hospital building, the entrance to Evergreen Cemetery
looks much the same today as it did in 1890, when this picture was taken. In that year, Capitol Hill residents looked for the spirits of the departed beyond the doors of their own haunted homes.
–Image courtesy of History Colorado Photograph Collection, #10038246
* * * * * * *

Citizen reports to the newspaper about unusual ghost lights in the cemetery continued and a larger expedition was mounted. On the designated night, the party returned to Evergreen to search the house further. It was a derelict structure previously used as a hospital by the Grand Army of the Republic and well fitted with old soldiers in spirit form. Once again, candles illuminated the upper-story windows, creating translucent images resembling ghosts clad in burial shrouds. Through the frosty windowpanes, the searchers saw a decorated Christmas tree. Pounding on the door, they received no response from either human or spectral inhabitants. One of the investigators tried to pick the lock, but was unsuccessful, and sentries, keeping a wary eye on the windows above, noticed someone blowing out the candles. They heard a gravelly female voice from within.

"What do you want?" it inquired.

"We thought the house was on fire," was the lying reply.

"Get out! Can't an old lady celebrate Christmas widout a lot of hoodlums trying to break in her dure?"

Convinced that the occupant had more human than spectral traits, the investigators left the graveyard and headed toward Capitol Hill with the eyes of the old lady peeping after them around one of the lacy curtains. When the searchers turned back for a final look at the "haunted" house, she realized she was discovered and jumped away from the window.

The house that was the subject of so much excitement was occupied by a man known as "Corporal" Casey, a character about town who worked as the building's caretaker and paid no rent for living there.

* * * * * *

"A poets graveyard has already been established, and the eight who lie there now hold in their little hands their 'Odes to Spring", which they tried to trade for mining stock and board. The cemetery is comfortably situated, and its inmates, so far, are quiet and inoffensive people. Send on your poets to Leadville."

--*The Solid Muldoon*, September 19, 1879

* * * * * *

Ghosts in the Graveyard, Etc.

HOW DEATH IS MET

"Collections of quaint epitaphs very often find their way into print; but how appallingly rich our language is in aphorisms on death, of all styles—serious, slangy and ghastly humorous.

'Indeed, every deceased person may be suited with an appropriate one, indicative of his profession, character and manner of death. Thus the polite man bids farewell to the world; the merchant closes his early accounts; the little child is received among the angels; the lamp-lighter has had his lamp of life extinguished; the wearied go to rest; the night watchman's hour of relief strikes; the sailor runs into harbor; the ferryman pays his fare to Charon; the reaper bites the grass; the gossip goes to the silent tomb; the grave digger sinks into the pit; the tippler's last draught is drawn; the watchmaker runs down; the unhappy breathe out their last sighs; the wanderer has gone to his home; the weaver's life-thread is cut by the fates; the bootblack goes to the shining land; the musician's wind has given out or his string has snapped; the dentist is filled in; the flutist pipes on his last note; the Jew rests in Abraham's lap; the smoker's pipe is put out; the sluggard goes to the land that knows no waking; the commission merchant is consigned to the dust; the nobleman is gathered to his fathers; the eyes of the inquisitive are closed by death; the scene-shifter 'shoves clouds;' the learned give up the ghost; the jockey has run his last race; the washerwoman has wrung out her spirit; the atheist has had to believe in it; the General has been transferred to the great army; the servant goes to meet his master; the Indian brave goes to the happy hunting-grounds; the hero has fought his last battle; the soldier has stacked his arms; the glutton must eat the dust; the butchers go the way of all flesh; the ticket agent passes in his checks; the Postoffice employee goes to the dead-letter office; the bloated bond-holder is called in; the banker is drawn on by death, and without recourse honors it; the jig dancer shuffles off his mortal coil; the linguist is translated to a better land; the distiller goes to the land of spirits; the tragedian makes his exit from the stage of life; the body-snatcher awaits the resurrection; the angler has at last become food for the worms; the loafer 'skips the gutter;' the florist goes where the woodbine twineth; the ice man stiffens up; the crockery man's vase is shattered; the clothier non-suited at last; the insurance man pays his last premium; the hod-carrier goes to the highest round; the printer's form is locked; the engineer's throttle is closed; the policeman is pulled to his narrow cell; the baseballist makes a home run; the Mormons go up to the Celestial Salt creek; the farmer is 'planted;' the lynched border man 'walks off a barrel, climbs a sapling, dances on air, or becomes cottonwood fruit, or is left kicking at the United States,' and lastly the confidence operator—well, he leaves for 'parts unknown'—but in the end they are all dead, just the same."

--Saguache Chronicle, June 14, 1879

* * * * * * *

Leadville's cemeteries are repositories for bones, where does the spirit wander after the final debt is paid?

* * * * * * *

"As he was walking, the usual turnip, white sheet and lanthorn of the conventional ghost were submitted to his gaze, with the customary weird howls. Tim, however, simply looked fixedly at the apparition for a moment and remarked: 'Arrah, now, and is it a general resurrection, or are ye just taking a walk by yerself?'"

—Littleton Independent, October 6, 1911, after Tim Casey's friends made plans to scare him at the churchyard on his way home late one night.

PADDY PLUNGES INTO THE PIT

In the early years of the 20th Century, a Leadville Irishman habitually took a shortcut through the graveyard on his way home from the tavern. Some of his friends, aware of his nightly route, concocted a scheme that would make for a good laugh. They found an old sunken grave along his customary path and dug it out, covering it with decaying boards so he would fall into the open pit when he crossed.

On the designated evening, his friends concealed themselves among the trees and waited. As expected, the Hibernian made his way along the cemetery trail and everything happened as planned. He came to the pitfall, crashed through the boards and disappeared into the yawning hole in the ground. While he was still in the bottom of the pit trying to make sense of what happened, his friends, dressed in white sheets and other ghostly vestments, emerged from the darkness and stood on the edge of the grave, peering down at the bewildered and terrified man.

"What are you doing in my grave?" asked one in a ghostly voice.

The question seemed to come from the very walls of the tomb itself, and made the Irisher's hair stand on end. He quickly gathered his wits and replied, "Faith, and what are you doing out of it?"

* * * * * * *

"With a tracking noise the coffin bursts
In the tomb, deep, dark and profound,
And the phantom white places his foot
On the soil of the cold, damp ground!
And the phantom white, whom the rushing rains
Had faded to a tint so fair,
Wiped with his shroud and his skeleton hand
The drops from his face and hair."

--Fort Collins Courier, December 21, 1893

* * * * * * *

FRIGHTFUL SIGHT AT ALBRIGHT'S

He finally gave it up, the mortician said to himself as he loaded the ghastly cargo that was Mr. Casey into the dead wagon, made a wide turn across Harrison Avenue in front of the Clarendon Hotel and began the sullen trip back to the embalming rooms. There, four moldering corpses awaited his attention: a prospector who succumbed to mountain fever, a Sooner whose heart stopped on Mosquito Pass, a dance hall girl who quaffed too much laudanum and an Austrian who was kicked in the forehead by a mule. It would be a busy night's work in the year 1899.

By morning, word of Casey's mysterious demise at the Tabor Opera House generally was known about town, and Mr. Stight, a 9 a.m. customer at Albright's Saloon on Harrison, sat at a table perusing the story in a Leadville tabloid. It was then that he looked up and saw Casey's corpse wander through the doors, go to the bar and ask for a drink. Stight was horrified to see the apparition of the dead man. After all, wasn't he asked to identify the body the previous day when Casey was laid out under a sheet in the lobby of the Clarendon?

Warily making their way to the bar, Stight and two Albright's employees confronted the spirit, who assured the group that he wasn't really in the post-mortal state.

"Prove it," said the skeptical barkeep, maintaining a safe distance from the ghost.

After reading about his demise in the newspaper, Casey said, he decided to come to Albright's for a celebratory drink. Turning away from the baffled men, he strode out of the saloon and walked the two blocks to the mortuary, where he asked to view his corpse. Studying the face of the man on the embalming table and realizing it wasn't him, he made his way back down the avenue, stopping at homes and businesses to inform his astonished friends of the miraculous resurrection.

Apparently, the dead man and Mr. Casey shared a remarkable resemblance and both bore the same last name. Later it was discovered that the cadaver was that of Henry Burke, commonly known by the alias "Casey."

Ghosts in the Graveyard, Etc.

"For some weeks the western declivity of Free Gold Hill, a little above town, has been the scene of a weird and fearful apparition. On the summit of one of the huge rocks in that locality, a little after midnight for several nights in succession, a female form is seen dressed in a white garment, with the deepest agony depicted on her countenance and waving a sword and pointing towards Buena Vista, exclaiming in a mournful and sepulchral voice accompanied with the moaning of the midnight zephyrs: 'Woe! Woe! Woe to the sinners!' A committee of spiritualists will shortly investigate the matter."

—Buena Vista Democrat, January 26, 1887

* * * * * * *

GHOST IN THE BOTTLES

Phantoms, either parched or just thirsting for human attention, were thought to be at the bottom of some early-morning fireworks at another Leadville saloon during March 1892. The Leadville Daily & Evening Chronicle followed up on the report of the strange doings at the barroom.

"A curious state of affairs existed Friday morning in a certain saloon on Harrison Avenue. Business was slow and the bartender settled himself in a chair near the fire and prepared to take a snooze. He had barely closed his eyes when an explosion, similar to the muffled report of a pistol, suddenly recalled him from the realms of Morpheus. He arose and looked around, but could find nothing unusual and returned to his chair. Within a few moments he fell asleep, another explosion was heard and the bartender again investigated, with the same result.

"He stood near the bar for a minute, when a cork from a soda bottle behind the bar struck the ceiling with a bang. Upon looking into the case of soda, he found that several bottles had bursted and the glass was lying in bits around the floor under the bar. Thinking the temperature of the room was too warm, he placed the remaining whole bottles in the ice box, but the bottles continued to burst until every one was gone. Several bottles of ginger ale also followed suit. By this time, hoboes who generally lounge around the place began to think that 'spooks' were abroad, and were not long in making their exit from the saloon."

Lower Harrison Avenue, especially near its intersection with Third Street, has a particularly dire history, and many a man took his dying breath in the vicinity. While most were victims of gunplay, one of the few exceptions to this rule was a townsman who dropped dead on the flagstones outside a Leadville tavern in 1884.

* * * * * * *

"Every twelfth night the dead walk. They sit too upon every tile of the house, waiting to be freed from purgatory by prayer."
—Aspen Daily Chronicle, October 2, 1889

* * * * * * *

'DEAD ENOUGH'

Meandering up Leadville's main street, the nameless pedestrian lay down on the sidewalk in front of the Streeter Saloon and gave up the ghost. Within minutes more than one hundred onlookers stood spellbound, peering down at the wonderfully strange spectacle of the corpse, which moments before was a living being.

"The crowd pressed hard to have the pleasure of looking a dead man in the face," said an early Leadville newspaper. "There was a respectful silence for an occasion of so much interest and delight."

Someone in the crowd found the nearest doctor, who leisurely arrived at the scene some time later. This prominent Leadville medicine man elbowed his way through the bystanders, briefly sized-up the cadaver and issued a verdict of "dead enough".

News that another mortal had cashed in his checks at the Streeter reached police headquarters, and Archie Walsh, the jailor, was the only man available to go and pick up the remains. Shouldering the well-used plank kept on hand for such occasions, Officer Walsh stepped onto the street, and followed by several hundred curious Leadvillites, made his way down Harrison Avenue as if guiding a flock of wayfarers on a pilgrimage to some holy shrine.

Walsh deposited the board respectfully alongside the dead man and recruited three onlookers to help him remove the stiff to the undertaking rooms. The two assistants at the dead man's feet and the others at the head exchanged uneasy glances and waited for Walsh's signal to lift the cadaver onto the bier. In an instant, the dead man jumped up and pummeled two of the pallbearers with his fists, knocking them to the ground. Twisting free from the other two, the unknown corpse shot down the street like a bolt from the blue, darted into an alleyway and disappeared into the thin Leadville air.

* * * * * * *

"In every age and in all climes, visitors hailing from beyond the mystic Styx are reported,"

—Herald Democrat, November 8, 1884

* * * * * * *

LURID LYRICS AT THE LIBERTY BELL

"If you had passed by the Liberty Bell Theater any time after midnight Monday," said the Carbonate Chronicle in January 1922. "You would have been concerned that the 'spooks' were holding an open house within."

Late-night passersby and neighbors were the first to notice something was amiss at the Liberty Bell when they were regaled with strains of unearthly music throughout the night. Mysterious melodies wafted from within the locked and darkened theater and onto the frozen avenue and dismal alleyway behind Harrison.

The phantom repertoire was diverse and included tunes of all types, ranging from weird, decadent minors and ragtime jazz to classical selections. No one could explain the music, and despite the cold, the otherworldly concert drew a small crowd that gathered near the front door and stayed until dawn began to brighten the eastern sky.

As quickly as it began, the music stopped with the arrival of daylight, and the loiterers were about to disperse when they heard the latch click and they turned to watch the theater door swing wide. Expecting to see some dark, phantom organist float through the entrance and glide down the avenue, what greeted their curious stares was anything but ghostly. Mr. Perkins, an employee of the Photo Player Company, which manufactured pianos for motion picture houses, stepped onto the frosty sidewalk and glared at the onlookers before turning to walk away.

Beginning at 10 p.m. the previous evening, he began tuning the Liberty Bell's organ, working throughout the night until early the next morning and producing the funereal midnight symphony that terrified neighbors.

"O you Knocker, depart from here hence. If thou be in the flesh come ye down and give battle, but if ye be a spirit get thee gone, before I reach the upper ramparts because if ye are a human, ye are about to die a frightful death, but if ye come from the land of spirits, I am about to evaporate into nothing."
—San Juan Prospector, February 19, 1916.
Challenge uttered by a homeowner when, during a ladies bridge party, a mysterious knocking was heard emanating from the upper story of the house.

* * * * * * *

BLIND MAN'S BLISS

During the early years of the 20th Century, mysterious screams, phantom hammering and unexplained lights in the abandoned Peck Building at the corner of East Sixth and Hemlock streets had that east-side neighborhood's Irish residents all atilt.

Nightly, especially as tipsy Hibernians checked out of local saloons, crowds gathered outside the derelict structure to witness the supernatural activity that emanated from within. Stouthearted railroad men, hardened teamsters and steely-nerved miners were seldom disappointed with their vigil before finally weaving a tipsified path home to regale their families with tales of the undead who walked the passageways of the old Peck place. Nobody was much surprised that a new crop of ghosts took up residence there, and the ghouls and their Irish neighbors peacefully coexisted for several years. After all, hadn't the wailing banshee, assorted sorceresses and unearthly women in black plagued the east-side neighborhoods for nearly three decades?

In 1901 a local newsman took an interest in the story.

Under the safety of the noonday sunshine, the writer entered the alley behind the structure and pushed open the old wooden gate leading through the tall grass to Peck's back door and knocked. Expecting his call to go unanswered, he wasted no time turning to walk away when the door squeaked open. In the entrance stood not some ghoulish resident of the netherworld, but Abe Lynn, who in days gone by owned a cigar and fruit stand on Chestnut Street.

Accepting an invitation to enter, the reporter followed his corporeal-looking host into the dim light of the decaying building to a sitting room furnished with a table, sofa and a rocking chair that groaned as its bespectacled owner sat down. The Turkish carpet covering the floor was stained with no small number of artistic patterns done in tobacco juice.

Revealing the purpose of the visit, the news writer said he intended to uncover the truth about the haunting. The blind man laughed and said he could shed some light on the ghostly fanfare. "Did you come armed?" asked Lynn. "I suppose you thought you would meet a monster with long horns and huge teeth."

Reaching into his coat pocket and brandishing only pad and paper, the scribe listened as the sightless man told his tale.

Thirty years earlier, Lynn continued, while prospecting in Idaho, an explosion in a mine sent him into eternal darkness. Doctors gave the injured man one day to live, but he recovered and came to Leadville with his sister.

"Since then I've been a victim of unrestrained happiness," he said, demonstrating the shout that paralyzed his neighbors. "There's not a happier man in the state than I. So whenever I wake in the night and roll over in bed, I feel so good with the world and everything in it that I just want to shout and sing a little. This is what they have heard."

Under this ghostly guise, the blind man lived in peace for years, fearing only that if the people learned the true nature of the noises, they would try to have him committed to an asylum. Lynn's sister, who ran a boarding house across the street, regularly delivered pies, cake and bread to the "ghost" of the Peck House. "The burros bray around all night and the drunk men sing," Lynn added. "I didn't think anyone would notice my shouts. As far as seeing a light, I haven't had one in here for years."

In his world of shadows, the man told the scribe, he intended to take the phantom clatter to another level because the curious crowds outside the Peck Building significantly increased the nearby saloon business. Lynn said he planned to procure some chains and old dishes with which to make a "terrible racket".

"And the liquor business will increase with the crowd. Then I will demand half of the profits and make a little money out of the 'ghost.'"

Completing the interview and pocketing his writing utensils, the reporter closed the back door, waded through the knee-high grass toward the alley gate and heard a hushed voice through a missing board in Peck's back door.

"Come again," it said. "But don't expect to find any ghosts."

* * * * * * *

"The belated wayfarer, who is traversing a low-lying church yard at 'the witching hour of midnight' sees, a short distance from him, a spectral presence hovering about the tombs, which his terrified imagination immediately regards as a disembodied spirit, a veritable ghost."

--Aspen Tribune, September 18, 1898

* * * * * * *

GHOSTLY MESSENGER FROM GOTHAM

Seated around a table in the office of the Hotel Kitchen during the fall of 1886, a skeptical group of friends asked a prominent Leadville mining man what made him believe that haunted houses were not the product of an overactive imagination.

"You can say what you blame please about spirits, but I am firmly convinced that such things exist," he told the group. "I had an experience in New York City four years ago that I wouldn't go through again for $5,000."

Among the assembled men was a Leadville reporter who, despite his distaste for such an unsavory subject, stayed to listen even though chills already were romping up and down his spinal column.

From the pocket of his coat the mine speculator produced a piece of paper on which was penned in a woman's hand, "Never mind the sale, but go home."

Examining the paper, the curious men listened as he explained how the message came into his possession.

In 1884, the storyteller said, he went to New York City to sell a mine. On the day he arrived, he met with the prospective buyers who said they would purchase the property on the spot if the paperwork were in order. Realizing their request would take several days of correspondence to complete, he took a room at a hotel near Madison Square and went to bed at 1 a.m. That night, the brooding storm over the city created a heavy, unpleasant atmosphere in the apartment.

Two hours later, the guest awoke and noticed a pale blue light filling the room, clearly illuminating the furnishings. Looking out the window, he saw a dark, empty street devoid of pedestrians and a lightning flash somewhere in the distance. Turning back towards the bed, the light became brighter and the mining man saw the figure of a woman materialize. She walked towards him as he stood frozen to the spot and unable speak. One step from the petrified man, the phantom reached out her hand and dropped a paper at his feet. At this, the lodger gave a terrified yell, the foggy visitor disappeared and the room faded to black. The bellboys heard the racket and ran to investigate.

"They finally concluded I was some poor idiot with the jim jams and left me alone in my glory," the mine seller told his audience.

On his way back to bed, he noticed the piece of paper that fell from the specter's hand, telling him to forgo the sale and return to Leadville. Knowing at once he needed to be in Colorado, he took the morning train and several days later was in the carbonate camp. Arriving home at 11 p.m., he opened the door and was met with a cloud of smoke from a lamp that was left burning and about to explode. He wrapped the smoldering light in a tablecloth, doused the flame and entered the bedroom where his wife and son slept soundly. The woman awoke at the sound of her husband's voice and asked why he returned home so soon. She laughed when he told her the tale of the ghostly messenger. "So you see gentlemen," the mining man told the listeners at the hotel office. "I lost the sale of the mine but saved the lives of my family."

* * * * * * *

"Ghosts? Why of course there are ghosts. Churchyards are full of ghosts. And no wonder churchyards are full of them. After he's been kicked and cuffed and abused all his life, where is the man whose ghost, especially on those balmy summer evenings, doesn't enjoy a quiet sit-down in the moonlight in order to read his epitaph."

—Littleton Independent, December 11, 1914

* * * * * * *

CHAPTER FIVE
SHADES OF THE RAILROAD GRADES

- Midland Station at Leadville-1885
Exactly how many people "departed" on the Midland is unknown, but the company's Lake County depot, yards and grades were particularly spook-infested, especially around the witching hour of midnight. Brakeman Butts attested to the fact; he saw the ghost roaming the yards one night in 1891. Image courtesy of History Colorado Photograph Collection, # 10038244

MIDSUMMER MAYHEM ON THE MIDLAND

Prominent Leadville residents met a nameless phantom known to stalk the area of the Midland rail yards early one morning in August 1892. A pair of city councilmen and others encountered the taciturn spook during their constitutional walk in the still hours before sunrise near the depot on West Third Street. Residents living nearby heard about the apparition and got their knickers in a twist at the thought of another supernatural entity roaming the neighborhood.

Gustav Erickson was the lucky Swede who encountered the

desolate specter of the rail yards early one Saturday morning as he ambled home at 4 a.m. While strolling by the Midland station, he was bewildered to see a white figure step out from behind the railcars standing on a siding, glide toward Chestnut Street and disappear from view. Erickson, a temperate man and also a firm believer in ghosts, bit down on his tongue and tweaked his ear to make sure he wasn't in dreamland.

After the figure vanished, Erickson stood staring, trying to make sense of what he just witnessed when two city councilmen happened along. When Gus told them about the phenomenon, one of the aldermen said something about him having too much to drink and urged him to go home. Erickson said he never touched ardent spirits, especially the Leadville variety.

Excited chatter between the men aroused the curiosity of several other people who gathered around to listen to the speculation on things supernatural. As they debated the subject of ghosts in Leadville, the phantom materialized again, drifting by a few feet south of the group and vanishing at the spot where it first appeared to the Swede. Witnesses were close enough to see the features of the spirit clearly, describing him as a tall man who passed them three feet above the ground. They placed his age at about 45 years and characterized him as handsome, with early gray hair. Wearing a sad, hunted expression, the ghost clutched a wound on his chest from which blood oozed.

When the ethereal being saw the men, it seemed troubled by their presence and changed its direction before vanishing from view. None of the spectators remembered any foul play that transpired in the area and they were unable to identify the apparition.

* * * * * * *

"Being killed while intoxicated caused the discontented spirit of the dead to return to the scene of his death."
—*Colorado Transcript*, December 14, 1887

* * * * * * *

Shades of the Railroad Grades

UNDER THE TABLE AND OVER THE RAIL

In the waning years of the 19th Century, fatalities on the railroad increased the shadowy ranks of the ghost-haunted Midland by three.

Archie Rose chose the wrong place to snooze, and even though his decapitated corpse went to rest peacefully in its stony tenement at Evergreen Cemetery, his headless, one-handed apparition returned to Leadville to walk the old Midland grade on the south side of town in the years following his death.

"With a whiskey bottle for a companion, he went to sleep on the railroad track," said the local headlines in a story detailing the demise of the 55-year old Scotsman.

Rose loved his liquor, and one summer night in 1899, he began his fateful journey down the Midland grade with bottle in hand, drunk as a fiddler. He hadn't floundered very far when he decided to recline next to the rails to sleep off the effects of the alcohol. Sometime later, a Colorado Midland work train, an engine and three flatcars returning to the Leadville, rounded the curve on its way to the Midland yards. It was running backwards down the grade and the engineer couldn't stop the heavy train by the time he saw Rose next to the tracks.

The rumble of the approaching cars roused the groggy man, who pulled himself up to sitting. The three cars passed and Rose toppled across the rail just before the locomotive reached him. The passing wheels sliced his head and one hand from the body, launching him on his eternal walk along the Midland grade.

* * * * * * *

"A man at the Midland depot was under the impression Friday night that he saw ghosts and monkeys in the freight rooms."

—Leadville Daily & Evening Chronicle, June 8, 1893

* * * * * * *

TRAGEDY ON THE TRESTLE

Occasionally seen, but more often heard laughing and playing on pleasant summer afternoons near the site of the Colorado Midland trestle that once soared across California Gulch, is the phantom of a boy who crossed the river of death there in a tragic accident in 1897.

Following the bigger neighborhood boys as they ventured from the safety of the neighborhood and crossed the massive span, five-year old Vincent Grey wanted to share the fun of climbing aboard the railcars that were standing atop the trestle. After playing for a short time, one of the youngsters thought a joke would add a thrill to the afternoon adventure.

"Run!" he shouted. "An engine's coming! Hurry up, an engine's coming!"

Even though there was no engine in sight, Vincent didn't realize it and started to scramble down from the flatcar on which he was playing. As he descended the ladder on the side of the car, his foot slipped, he lost his hold on the rungs and fell. His body struck a beam protruding from the trestle and plummeted 75 ft. to the rocky ground below. Several men tending the sheep yards nearby saw the boy plunge from the trestle and ran to help but found the lad already beyond hope in the grip of death.

Today, the trestle is gone, but clad in immortality, young Vincent still enjoys his creekside boyhood adventures along California Gulch where the trestle once carried the Midland trains to and from the depot.

Some 30 years later, he found a playmate.

During the second decade of the 20th Century, hard economic times fell on Leadville and coal was an important commodity that was difficult for many families to afford. It was a common practice for children to walk along the railroad grades picking up coal that fell from passing trains.

One group of siblings was scouring the rails and searching the empty coal cars standing along the steep slope of Brooklyn Heights in 1928, when one of the youngsters found a particularly large, round lump of fuel lying in the bottom of a car. Tossing it over the edge, it dropped to the ground and rolled away. Gaining more speed as it traveled, the rock bounced its way down the hill. Before it reached the bottom of the gulch, the speeding lump of anthracite became airborne and struck an 11-year old girl in the head, killing her instantly and whisking her into the presence of Vincent Grey and others who still frolic in the water and gold-bearing sands of California Gulch.

"About 10 o'clock last night Conrad Heineman, a son of the county surveyor, was practicing foot racing on Ohio street. He wore only his underwear, and a barber named Charley Davis shot him in the hip. The bullet ranged up into the bowels and recovery is considered doubtful. Davis, who is now under arrest, says he thought it was a ghost."

—*Leadville Daily & Evening Chronicle*, November 2, 1894

* * * * * * *

BEWARE THE BOULEVARD

Early visitors to the west side of the Upper Arkansas Valley and its popular soda spring resorts originally made their way to the foot of Mt. Massive via a crooked and dangerous road called "Lunatics Lane" because it was said that one had to be crazy to drive it. The springs became so popular that a new route, christened "The Boulevard" was built, straight as a pin westward from Leadville to where it spanned the Arkansas River.

Travelers heading west on Third Street topped the hill above City Cemetery and coasted westward down the Boulevard through a corridor of lodgepole pines, crossed the river and passed the fragrant, sage-covered flats before arriving at their destination. The new road was completed in late 1880 and its 60-foot width was kept smooth as velvet and dust-free by constant care.

The Leadville and Soda Springs Omnibus and Toll Road Company managed the road and operated vehicles along its length, including a large passenger wagon, horse-drawn taxis and vehicles fitted with water tanks for sprinkling the road during the dusty high-country summer. Travel to and from the Soda Springs Resort was constant—day and night and year-round, and tolls brought in $15 a day from wagons loaded with freight, wood, ore and sightseers. Daily hack service between Leadville and Soda Springs began in 1882.

Railroad grades crossed The Boulevard in several places—just west of the hilltop and again two miles beyond, near the upper end of Malta Gulch. Evening travelers familiar with the rueful history of these crossings hurried on their journey a little faster and pulled their coats more tightly around them as they warily passed these spook-ridden junctions.

In November 1886, a work party started from Leadville one evening destined for the Hagerman Tunnel. One man rode a horse, driving a mule ahead of him. Starting west on The Boulevard, the journey was uneventful until he reached the point where the Denver & Rio Grande tracks crossed it.

As the party approached the crossing, the horse stopped dead in its tracks and the rider felt the hair on the broomtail's back and neck stand up. Seeing nothing, the man was bewildered at the animal's behavior as it stood there shivering. Despite the urging of the rider, the horse wouldn't advance. Peering into the semi-darkness he saw something crouching on the track in front of him, and in the waning light he discerned the figure of a woman, completely shrouded except for the eyes. The rider spoke to the figure, asking her name but the phantom rose up, glided down the track and disappeared into the twilight.

Dwelling on the strange encounter, the worker shuddered with the eerie feeling that he just encountered a spirit on the lonely road. What he saw was the tormented specter of a deranged woman who met an untimely end at the crossing several years earlier.

* * * * * * *

Shades of the Railroad Grades

At this lonely spot along "The Boulevard" in 1882, an insane woman flung herself beneath the wheels of a passing train. Following her gruesome demise, travelers along the road often encountered her unquiet, drifting soul.

* * * * * * *

Marie Royer's troubled spirit took up residence in the sulfide camp in 1882. After running away from the county poor house in Malta, she was killed by a train near the spot where The Boulevard intersected the D&RG tracks. The emotion of her distraught condition apparently was enough to compel her ghost to remain at the crossing, caught somewhere between life and death, searching for the husband she believed would return for her.

Mrs. Royer was mentally unstable when her husband Samuel committed her to the indigent home in the summer of 1882. Her condition didn't permit him to care for her and keep a job, and he didn't earn enough to pay for her room and board at an asylum. At the poor house, Samuel told the matron that his wife would be staying a short time and that he would return soon to take her to more suitable accommodations. Marie was content at her new home for one day before becoming uncontrollable, saying she was leaving to look for her husband. Donning her cloak and cap, she headed for the door, where the superintendent stopped her.

"There was a struggle, but it did not last long," the newspaper reported. "The woman being strong and nerved with the insane idea that she must go, struggled as only a mad woman can struggle. She, by sheer force, broke away from the hands of her captor and sped away like a deer."

Later that day, acquaintances spotted Marie in Leadville on Harrison Avenue and in the evening at a house along the Boulevard Road, where she told the occupants she was looking for Samuel. A pair of men on their way to Soda Springs encountered the woman near a rail crossing but didn't stop to speak with her. Alone and plagued by the demons in her mind, Mrs. Royer sat down between the rails to await destruction.

Minutes later, a train running uphill under full steam roared around the bend below the crossing. Despite the sound of the bell, Marie sat motionless on the tracks as the engineer set the brakes, stopping the train just before it struck her. The fireman jumped down to talk with the woman but she stood up, refused to speak and hurried away.

Returning from Soda Springs, the two men who saw her earlier in the day spotted her again. Refusing their offers for help and paying no attention to their directions back to the city, Marie wandered away and disappeared into the forest. They were the last to see her alive, and early the next morning a D&RG freight train cut her to ribbons when she threw herself under the wheels of the passing cars. The conductor, riding in the caboose, was the first to discover her segmented remains scattered along 150 ft. of track. Police and the coroner went to the scene and used sticks and sacks to collect the gore.

In the years leading up to her grisly end, Mrs. Royer's mental condition deteriorated steadily after her second marriage in 1870 and the weddings of her daughters. She adopted the habit of fleeing the house in her nightgown and running through the snow, frantic with worry for the welfare of her children in Denver. On at least one other occasion she tried to enlist in the army of ghosts and goblins beneath the wheels of a train but an alert Leadville policeman intervened before she jumped.

Marie Royer's memory was forgotten to history, and time

and the elements have given The Boulevard a new look. Once groomed and dust free, it is now in a sad state of disrepair, rough and rutted from rain, snow and lack of upkeep. What remains unchanged from 1882 is the ghost of Marie Royer, who still startles the occasional traveler at the haunted rail crossing in the twilight forest along the Boulevard Road.

* * * * * * *

"It is said that a $500 reward will be offered for the return of the young lady who was frightened by ghosts on the Boulevard the other evening."
—Carbonate Chronicle, July 8, 1889

* * * * * * *

MAUDLIN ON THE MAIN LINE

In 1897, one more ghost joined those already lingering at the Boulevard's forbidding railroad crossings.

Albert Richmond drank on the job while working as a carpenter at the Arkansas Valley Smelter near Stringtown. During the spring of that year, he and his fellow framers were busy erecting a new oven for the roasting of ore. Hard, dusty work and the contents of the bottle in his coat left the man fatigued and giddy by the time the shift whistle sounded late one afternoon early in March.

* * * * * * *

While yet a boy, I sought for ghosts and sped
Through many a listening chamber, cave and ruin
And starlight wood, with fearful footsteps pursuing
Hopes of high talk with the departed dead.
—Percy Bysshe Shelley
Hymn to Intellectual Beauty

* * * * * * *

Shades of the Railroad Grades

- Arkansas Valley Smelting Co. building--1900
Ore processing was hot, dusty, dangerous work and Leadville's many smelters did their share to keep the undertakers employed and the phantoms moaning. Pots of molten slag, spinning gears and the weighty stamps that pulverized rock to dust killed and maimed many employees, as did the belated death that came from years of inhaling poisonous, lead-laden smelter smoke.
Image courtesy of History Colorado Photograph Collection, # 10038243

* * * * * * *

Leaving the smelter, Richmond and a fellow worker named Gillis meandered an unsteady path along the Rio Grande tracks towards town, despite the objections of their fellow workers who suggested they hire a wagon to take them safely home. The pair ignored the advice and stumbled along the grade, Gillis in the lead, when a passenger train approached from behind the drunken men. At the sound of the whistle, Gillis stepped off the rails but when Richmond tried to jump out of the way he fell back into the path of the oncoming engine. The impact tore the man's scalp from his head and the wheels crushed his shoulder and severed both legs below the knees. Life quickly ebbed out of his body and the smelterman quit the world to join the phantom rabble on the railroad.

Legless at the end of his life, the gory but reassembled specter of Albert Richmond still weaves an errant and horrible trail along the abandoned rail bed between Stringtown and Leadville in the gruesome re-enactment of his death march on the Rio Grande.

Shades of the Railroad Grades

"There are lots of folks who have an aversion to ghosts, but those who like spirits are in the majority."

—*Littleton Independent, August 2, 1895*

* * * * * * *

LUNAR LARCENY

As with the haunted Midland Depot west of Harrison Avenue, the Denver & Rio Grande passenger station, formerly located on the northeast side of Leadville, offered its own cast of spectral characters. Among them was a menacing highwayman whose visits apparently were dictated by the lunar phases.

Every time the moon changed, said a D&RG conductor and a pair of brakemen in 1891, the road agent from the spirit land strode into Caboose No. 418, bristling with guns and knives as if to relieve passengers of their cash and baubles. Those employees unfortunate enough to be on the car at the time made a mercurial exit at the appearance of the dire entity, and even though the lifeless bandit never waylaid or injured anyone, it left witnesses terror-stricken every time.

Rail workers believed the phantom to be that of a late-unlamented member of a gang of train holdups that plied their trade in the vicinity soon after the railroad arrived in 1880.

Several years later, the shade of a rejected young woman who never lived to see her wedding day haunted the area around the Denver, South Park and Pacific passenger depot.

* * * * * * *

"The Cottage is the solitary place of habitation in Strawberry gulch, and in the region of the hanging ground upon which three felons have said good-bye to the world forever…These executions are what makes Strawberry gulch a prominent spot in the mountains, and it is not strange that the imps should return to make life interesting."

—*An 1886 Leadville newspaper*

* * * * * * *

WRONGED BY THE WHEELRIGHT

Green-eyed jealousy resulting in death was fertile ground from which many of Leadville's restless souls sprang. An untimely demise while caught up in such an all-consuming emotion often resulted in the dead carrying their unfinished affairs into the next world, compelling them to return to the realm of the living to set things right.

"The dictations of the human heart are mysterious, indeed, as when the passion of jealousy is once aroused there is no telling to what extreme the supposed injured party will resort," said a Leadville newsman as a series of bizarre events unfolded in the city during the eighth decade of the 19th Century.

Leadville was in its rough-and tumble youth when Mamie Rozier came to the carbonate camp from Kansas to look for gainful employment. Being as comely as she was cultured, her moral fiber rejected the seduction of State Street's easy vices and she found work at a hotel several blocks from the anarchy of lower Harrison Avenue and its wayward sisters, State and Chestnut.

Among the hotel boarders were three workingmen: a teamster, an ore-sorter and a wheelright, all of which took an immediate fancy to Mamie. Each was set on winning the woman's hand but the wheelright persevered and attained the desired result. Before long, the woman quit her job at the hotel but didn't loosen the grasp on her suitor. Instead, she spent most of her time daydreaming about what she believed would be her upcoming engagement and marriage. The wheelright, on the other hand, suffered from weak knees and curtailed his visits, eventually dropping Mamie completely.

Claiming he promised to marry her, the hotel girl wasn't easily abandoned and she threatened to kill him and herself if he refused to make the trip to the altar. Settling their differences after exchanging a love letter or two, the couple enjoyed a temporary make-up, but the wheelright's attentions once again cooled to less than tepid.

One afternoon, when Mamie chanced to see her Lothario strolling down the avenue with another female, she became so frenzied that she went home, procured a hefty revolver and went looking for the pair, forecasting a double murder and suicide. On another occasion when her jaundiced eye caught them leisurely glissading along Harrison, Mamie followed the lovebirds to the woman's house and waited outside in ambush until the early morning hours. The man spotted his former sweetheart hovering in the shadows, and suspecting that a hail of lead likely awaited him on the street, the wheelright made his getaway through the outhouse and into the alley. Over the next several days, Miss Rozier also showed up unexpectedly at his shop on East Sixth Street but never found him on the job adjusting the town's off-kilter wagon wheels.

- Railroad car at Leadville about 1890
Green-eyed jealousy drove a pretty hotel employee to the rail yards to search for her sweetheart, but her name was added to the rolls of Leadville's restless dead when she was killed one night beneath the wheels of a passenger car.
Denver Public Library Western History Collection, X-6372

* * * * * * *

Refusing to be rebuffed, Mamie turned her attention in the direction of the Denver, South Park & Pacific depot, daily making a close study of the passengers on each departing train, consumed by the suspicion that her lost lover might be among them. At night, she carried a lantern along the tracks, inspecting the travelers' faces through the windows of the cars. Her obsession ended abruptly one evening while attempting to cross the rails in between coaches. The train suddenly lurched, and knocking her onto the track, the unforgiving wheels sliced her into three pieces. One of the fragments, usually the one holding the lantern, still faithfully appears in the darkness on the anniversary of her demise, floating to and fro around the site of the once busy old railyards.

STANDARD ORE BUCKETS, CORNISH KIBBLES

BANKS, MORSE & Co

These buckets are made of steel pressed into shape. They are smooth outside with countersunk rivets The bottoms are dished so that the ring does not prevent them from standing upright.

No.	Height.	Diameter.			No Steel.	Capacity.		Weight	Price With Band.	Price Without Band.	Price Extra for Strips on Side.
		Top.	Center.	Bottom.		Cubic Feet.	Av. Lbs. Ore.				
1	30	21	24	17	9	6¼	750	140	.....	$23.00	$4.00
2	30	21	24	17	11	6½	750	125	$19.00	.....	4.00
3	32	24	27	21	8	9	1100	195	30.00	28.00	6.00
4	37	28	34	23	¼	15	1700	400	62.00	58.00	8.00
5	37	24	28	22	¼	11	1300	350	48.00	45.00	7.00
6	24	20	22	16	14	4½	550	67	12.00	.....	3.00
6½	28	20	24	16	14	6	725	75	15.00	.....	3.50
7	19	17	19	14	16	2½	300	35	10.00	.....	2.00
10	40	27	32	23	¼	15½	1800	400	64.00	60.00	8.00
11	48	26	31	22	¼	17½	2100	425	67.00	65.00	10.00
12	40	26	31	22	¼	14½	1650	375	52.00	50.00	7.00
13	42	26	31	22	⅛	15	1700	385	54.00	52.00	8.00
14	28	22	28	19	3/16	7½	900	150	27.00	25.00	4.00

A complete stock of all these sizes always on hand ready for immediate shipment. Other sizes and weights made to order. Prices on application. Any of the sizes given can be made of any weight of steel.

CHAPTER SIX
SPIRITS IN THE SHADOW OF MT. MASSIVE

- Leadville & Mt. Massive-1915
Magnificent beyond description is the Sawatch Range, whose ramparts form the Continental Divide west of Leadville. Mt. Massive, the northernmost sentinel on the range, has witnessed the insignificant comings, goings and ghostly returnings of human beings ever since they first migrated into these alpine valleys.
Denver Public Library Western History Collection, #00138320

A PROPER WELCOME

Mining in one form or another took place in nearly every canyon slicing into the flanks of Mt. Massive. From Twin Lakes on the south to Hagerman Pass on the north, prospectors investigated Half Moon, Willow, Rock, Busk and Lake Fork creeks on the eastern slope and the Ivanhoe and Fryingpan drainages on the west.

Most of the mining activity centered on the Leadville side of Sugar Loaf Mountain. Seekers of wealth on its heights pulled gold, silver and zinc ore from mines such as the New Discovery, Silver Moon, Black Iron, Golden Curry, Orinoco and Buckeye State mines and the Dinero Tunnel at the base of the mountain. On its slopes saloons, stores and boardinghouses provided miners with life's necessities, and cabins scattered along roads that crisscrossed Sugar Loaf provided living quarters for many more residents.

Anxious to hit a paying mine, some of the diggers in the district even looked to the ghostly realm for directions to rich deposits of ore

"The spirits of the other world are also greatly interested in mining," said a Leadville news writer in 1900. "In fact, there must be a small army of these airy beings who do nothing else but act as controls for professional mediums, and the latter are so generous and open-hearted that for the mere pittance of a dollar or so, they will tell where to find a million-dollar mine."

Every clairvoyant who set foot in Leadville did a thriving business and many a prospector, weary of fruitless digging, didn't hesitate to consult the beings from beyond the veil. One pretty wine-lugger turned "seer" quit her job at the Grand Central Theater to offer psychic advice to prospectors. For a nominal fee of five dollars, she dropped into a trance during which she could see the future and tell where the wealth was to be found in the surrounding mountains, giving precise coordinates of rich deposits of mineral.

"The best part of the story is that she poor girl is making piles of money from her five dollar fool fishing fees," reported an 1880 Leadville newspaper.

During 1899, when the Twin Lakes District showed promise, ghostly advisers told a local medium that rich ore was at hand but some digging would be necessary before the vein was uncovered. As a result, a mining partnership was formed and work progressed with unwavering faith in the counsel of the spirit miners.

In another case, a Leadville barber named Rosendorf squandered his entire savings on spiritualistic advice regarding where to dig at his claim in Empire Gulch. Opening a tunnel, it drifted into the hill with more zigs and zags than the road over Independence Pass.

"One medium would receive word from the ghostly land to turn the drift in a certain direction," the newspaper said. "Then another white-winged adviser would countermand the order and off the tunnel would go in another direction until finally between the host of spirits, Rosendorf's tunnel broke into the open air about 300 feet from the mouth after worming its way into the hill for considerable distance."

In 1898, reports reached Leadville from the Sugar Loaf Mining District that Martin Tiernan, another confirmed spiritualist, was losing his mind after prospectors noticed him acting in a most peculiar manner. They became concerned when they spotted him one morning standing precariously atop the headframe of the Reed National Shaft waving his arms as if taking part in some type of strange ritual. On another occasion, miners returned to their cabins to find their homes had been entered and certain possessions stolen. It was then that they realized the wheels had finally come off Tiernan's ore car.

Organizing a search party, the miners went to the man's residence and found their missing cookware and blankets neatly stacked around the room. When questioned about the thefts, Marty said he took their belongings because he expected visitors from the spirit world who would announce where the gold was to be found. He wanted enough bedding and dinnerware on hand to make the tired and hungry otherworldly pilgrims feel welcome, he told his associates.

To further entice his ghostly guests, Tiernan caught a neighbor's horse, harnessed and readied the animal and cinched it to a tree outside his cabin. He claimed he had to furnish his visitors from the netherworld with proper transportation during their sojourn on the mountain.

Tiernan's ghosts apparently never arrived with their map to the mother lode but scores of Sugarloaf residents appeared in Leadville and purchased every hasp and padlock in town.

Who did wander into the district was an eastern mining engineer with ambitious plans to unlock the geological treasure vault beneath Sugar Loaf. His spirit reportedly wanders the mountain wilderness to this day.

Spirits in the Shadow of Mount Massive

"Where there once stood two hundred houses in Malta, there are now fourteen. But then Malta has a haunted dwelling, and perhaps that makes up for the other deficiencies."

—Leadville Daily & Evening Chronicle, July 25, 1889

YE MINING EXPERT

A spectacled goose, from college let loose,
Said: "A mining expert I will be;
I'll examine all mines in the bowels of earth,
And some that are under the sea;
Don't you see?
And some that are under the sea.
"For I know all things that are to be known
Of science called ge-ol-o-gee;
By which I'll show people just how to get rich,
And charge them a comfortable fee;
Don't you see?
And charge them a comfortable fee.
"But hold! I've heard that miners out west
Bamboozle such fellows as we—
And I think it is best that I live there awhile,
For they may come their tricks over me;
Don't you see?
For they may come their tricks over me."
So to Sugar Loaf camp he fled him in haste,
This master of ge-ol-o-gee;
But the natives thought he was very low grade,
And they hanged him right up in a tree;
Don't you see?
And they hanged him right up in a tree.
Then the death-angel dropp'd this spectacled youth—
Setting his bright young spirit free—
And I'm told he's out now with a ghostly crew,
Prospecting all eternity;
Don't you see?
Prospecting all eternity.

--From an early Leadville newspaper

"But all these things might have been endured had not the ghost of the headless miner appeared. It has frequently been seen by the miners in the various drifts. It walks about the mine at all seasons, and no one knows when he will meet him or glance over his shoulder to see the headless one standing close behind him."

—Carbonate Chronicle, May 13, 1901

NECKTIE PARTY'S GRIM GHOST

As was the custom during the winter months, most of the prospectors and miners on the heights of the Sawatch Range left for warmer climes, said a local newspaper—"only those of remarkable fortitude undertaking to resist the tempests and biting elements. Nor do these do much promenading off the path between the shaft house or the tunnel's mouth to the weather-beaten cabin."

In the spring, the more sensible claim owners trickled back to their cabins and the rumble of dynamite was again heard throughout the area.

As the May sunshine began to eat away the snow pack, miners on the alpine slopes of Mt. Massive began telling uncanny tales of strange apparitions during the spring of 1887. Charlie Eldridge, a respected prospector from Leadville and numerous other reliable miners vouched for the veracity of the manifestations.

Early one morning, Mr. Eldridge came to Leadville before the sun began to thaw the snow. Beginning his journey at 3 a.m., he moved along at a rapid pace when he looked up to see an unbelievable and terrifying apparition. Floating along beside him was the white figure of a man dressed in the style of a miner. Eldridge took a belt from the flask he carried in his pocket and noticed that the apparition had a shabby, blood-caked beard and eyeballs that protruded from their sockets. Raising its right hand, the phantom ripped a knotted piece of rope from around his neck and flung it to the ground in disgust before vanishing into the darkness.

"I never felt so much relief in all my life as when the object disappeared, and I found myself breathing as if the demon itself had throttled me. I don't believe in ghosts, but I'll swear to this vision, and open myself to teachings," Eldridge said.

Back at his cabin, Mr. Eldridge told his companions about the experience and the miners organized a nightly vigil to watch for the apparition.

According to the old-timers in the area who came in quest of placer gold, a gentleman of questionable character was taken by vigilantes and hung from a rail that was placed between the notches of two pine trees.

In 1887, the newspaper said, the makeshift gallows was still in place.

"It was the victim of this necktie party who had probably returned to heap his wrath on his successors and baptize the gulch in his maledictions."

The grave of the murdered man was near the spot where Mr. Eldridge met the unwanted traveling companion. In the months following the sighting, miners going to Leadville or returning to Sugar Loaf never failed to make the journey during daylight hours, thus hoping to avoid a pre-dawn encounter with the strangled spook.

* * * * * * *

"Malta has a ghost which delights in scaring the members of the community who are tardy in wending their way homeward. The identity of his or her ghostship has not yet been determined, but George Clark and a few other of the boys are engaged in preparing a surprise party, which George asserts will either kill, lay or scare the ghost, or make spiritualists of himself and confreres."
—*Leadville Daily Herald*, November 1, 1882

* * * * * * *

Spirits in the Shadow of Mount Massive

- Mines on Sugar Loaf Mountain

Many people lived and died at Sugar Loaf Mountain during their search for the mineral riches it held. Some joined their ancestors as a result of gunshot wounds, fatal falls, giant powder explosions, snow slides and falling trees. Strange lights visible on the mountain at night give rise to speculation that spirits of the dead still walk the earth there.

* * * * * * *

"Ghosts that tramp the midnight air—ghosts in every thoroughfare— ghosts that haunt the weary brain—ghosts of living, ghosts of slain— ghosts that always have been found trespassing on troubled ground."

--Silverton Standard, June 8, 1907

* * * * * * *

DEATH BENEATH THE DIVIDE

During the 1880s, Colorado Midland Railroad management was looking at a way to link the Upper Arkansas and Roaring Fork valleys. The solution was to drive the Hagerman Tunnel beneath the Continental Divide at the stratospheric elevation of 11,528 feet and complete a rail connection between Colorado Springs and Aspen.

Opened in 1887, the tunnel was 2,064 feet long, its eastern approach featuring 16-degree curves, four-percent grades, snowsheds and a magnificent trestle. Financial difficulties and the cost of snow removal ate the profits and rail traffic through the Hagerman was discontinued several years later with the opening of another tunnel 600 ft. below in more hospitable climes.

Crews began driving the Busk-Ivanhoe Tunnel from both sides of the divide in 1890, and the first train steamed through the mountain three years later. At a length of 9,400 feet and a cost of $2 million, the project was marked by fatality and dozens of men lost their lives during tunnel construction.

In 1919, the last engine made the run between Busk Creek and Ivanhoe, and the tunnel was closed forever to trains. When the rails and ties were removed, the long bore was renamed. In 1925, it was opened to automobile traffic when Elizabeth McCarthy of Glenwood Springs smashed a bottle of ginger ale on the timbers of the western portal and christened it the Carlton Highway. Since it was too narrow to permit cars to pass inside the mountain, traffic signals were installed at either end and travel changed direction every 30 minutes.

* * * * * * *

- Colo. Midland engine at Ivanhoe about 1900
Driving a railroad tunnel was just like mining—drilling, blasting and mucking, except tunnelers didn't have to spend their time sorting ore. Construction of the Busk-Ivanhoe Tunnel was tainted with death; moving railcars, bad air, caving ground and explosions exacted a lethal toll. When the last rail spike was hammered in 1893, this Midland engine and others like it could pierce the Continental Divide through the Busk's 9,400 feet of more or less solid rock.
Denver Public Library Western History Collection, R.H. Kindig, Z-5330

* * * * * * *

In February 1892, there was an accident at the Busk-Ivanhoe Tunnel in which a project foreman named John Roach was crushed by a fall of rock early one afternoon as the men returned to work from dinner.

On that fateful day, Roach, nicknamed "Yorkie", entered the Busk from the western end and walked to the face of the drift where work was progressing through a section of unstable ground. The progress called for close timbering but the lagging wasn't in place when tons of dirt and rock fell on the foreman, crushing him to the floor. Roach's companions dug him out in fatally injured condition and complaining of pain in his arms and legs. Death came several agonizing hours later.

The tunnel pump operator, known only as Dan, told what happened to him after the accident.

In March, Dan crossed the valley to Leadville, money in hand, to have a few drinks with friends. After several glasses, his tongue loosened and he began to talk freely, but between periods of lucid speech he seemed to sink into deep thought. When the bartender asked what was going through his mind during his reveries, Dan made the barkeep promise never to repeat what he was about to hear.

"There's something on my mind that's been bothering me for a long time," he said. "You're the first person I've ever told."

After "Yorkie" died, Dan told the barkeep, most of the crew took the day off out of respect for the unfortunate man, but Dan the pump man had to remain at the tunnel to keep the water from rising too high in the workings. At 1 a.m., he took a candle, entered the drift and walked to the pump station, where he found everything working as it should. Dan stood there leaning against the humming machine when he noticed several shadows approaching from the heading. Surrounded by ice-cold air, Dan was amazed as he watched, frozen to the spot with fear. The shadowy figures materialized into a funeral procession led by a priest in robes carrying an open bible. Six dusky human forms carrying a coffin passed in front of Dan. As they did, one of the figures let go of the handle, stepped to one side and passed between Dan and the pump against which he was leaning.

After the phantom pallbearer passed, it took hold of the casket again. Dan followed the death procession until he was outside the tunnel, where the figures walked across the dump and disappeared into the darkness. The pump man returned to the tunnel and asked the engineer who also was working that night if saw anything unusual. He said no, but asked why Dan was sweating and looked so pale. The pump man evaded the question and said nothing for weeks until he came to Leadville and spoke with the bartender.

* * * * * * *

"People who are loudest in declaring there are no 'spooks' could not be driven into a so called 'haunted' house with a club."
—Aspen Democrat, September 30, 1910

* * * * * * *

Spirits in the Shadow of Mount Massive

- Busk–Ivanhoe Tunnel with cars-1929
Converting this tunnel from rail to automobile traffic saved drivers the jolting, rockbound ride over Hagerman Pass, especially in 1920s-vintage motorcars like these. Had motorists known the morbid history of the tunnel, they might have preferred potholes to ghosts.
Denver Public Library Western History Collection, # 00007261

STONE-DEAD AT ST. KEVIN

Six miles from Leadville and a short distance north of Turquoise Lake, St. Kevin Gulch plunges down a heavily timbered cleft and opens onto the sage-covered expanse of Tennessee Park. Thomas Walsh discovered the St. Kevin vein in 1883 and during the last decades of the 19th Century, mining operations there produced silver in quantities such that a small settlement grew up around the St. Kevin Mine. The big dreams weren't realized and by 1900, the area was abandoned.

"Dilapidated shaft houses, deserted dwellings, charred ruins of old mills and other evidences of departed glory greet the observer on every hand on St. Kevin Mountain," said the Denver Times in 1901. "Grass now grows in the beaten paths that were lined with miners and vigorous prospectors, who fancied that millions were awaiting their energies. Hundreds of tons of twisted iron bars, steel stamps and great castings from giant machines mark the locations of quartz mills, and long tram tracks tell of the mode of transporting the ore from the mines. Scores of little tunnels worm their way into the hills from the bottom of gulches where the absence of dumping room signifies the short distance the old time miners intended to go before opening the Eldorados."

Paying the most dividends in the St. Kevin District was the mine of the same name. It was there in 1887 that Albert Smith, the mine's engineer, was fatally injured in an early-morning boiler explosion that broiled him, sent him on a 150-yard aerial voyage and leveled the mine's shaft house. He went to rest quietly in the grave, but a St. Kevin miner who was killed in the shaft three years later wasn't so quick to go to his final reward.

Charles Toumar, a native of Finland, left his wife and two children in the old country to come to America and find his boulder of gold. Lake County looked promising so he settled down and started digging. He and his partner were busy sinking the St. Kevin Shaft beyond its timbered depth of 375 ft. during the day shift in the summer of 1890. The night crew miners set off their blasts and were climbing out of the shaft as Toumar and his companion rode the bucket to the bottom of the mine. The foreman warned them to check the spaces between the timbers on the way down in case any rocks came to rest there after blasting. The two men, engaged in lively conversation, didn't do a close examination and went directly to work.

After looking over the previous night's labor, Toumar stayed underground while his partner went to the surface for drills. Returning to the worksite with the sharpened steel, the miner stepped off the bucket and found the fallen body of the Finlander, head crushed and brains scattered over the surrounding rocks. Evidently, as the bucket rose to the surface, a stone weighing several pounds was knocked from where it rested on a timber, and falling from a great height, landed directly on the man's head.

Such a sudden mortal blow left Toumar's essence somewhat confused at the bottom of the shaft. Believing he was still at work in fleshly form, he carried on with the task of mining in spirit until finally realizing he was numbered with the dead. In the days and weeks following the accident, the chilling, from-the-bottom-of-a-well sound of the dead miner's voice emanated from the walls of the mine, usually during shift changes, warning the workers to check for rocks shaken loose during blasting.

* * * * * * *

Tucked into an isolated corner of Tennessee Park, St. Kevin Gulch once was home to many people: musicians, miners, merchants, mule-shoers and milliners. All left town when the silver gave out, leaving the ruins to assorted merry-makers of the spectral variety.

* * * * * * *

"A skeptical age; we do not believe in much of anything—unless, indeed, it bears the trademark of science…and yet, says Everybody's Magazine—the paradox is curious—never was the world so ghost-ridden. Never has it turned so wistfully to the occult. Never has it listened with an expectation so painful, at that closed door behind which mysterious silences stretch away—the door of the tomb."

--Morning Times, December 6, 1895

* * * * * * *

Prospecting Plant

CHAPTER SEVEN
UNDERGROUND APPARITIONS
* * * * * * *

- Miners descending in bucket-1880

Riding in an open bucket to and from the depths of the mine was a quick, convenient way to access the underground workings. During the dark, dizzying trips up and down the shaft, Death in its most hideous forms was the unseen, ever-present passenger. Ghostly workers in the Moyer, Mikado and Morning Star mines also were known to climb aboard buckets, taking this everyday practice to a supernatural level.
Denver Public Library Western History Collection, #10011636

* * * * * * *

Underground Apparitions

What more atmospheric setting for a ghost story than a mine? Damp, dark and silent, the claustrophobic confines of the underground workings were not unlike the tomb, a place where humans came face-to-face with their own mortality.

During the last two decades of the 19th Century, hundreds of Lake County miners answered the final summons at the worksite. Falls, explosions, caving ground, moving cars, falling objects and hoisting accidents accounted for a large share of Death's subterranean harvest. Exactly how many of their number returned in spirit form to work another graveyard shift isn't known, but the eeriness of ghosts in the workings ebbed, flowed and shivered throughout the Leadville Mining District as long as the mines continued to operate. Not surprisingly, the bizarre environment underground was flush with all varieties of fantastic creatures, including pranksome pixies, wailing banshees and mischief-loving fairyfolk.

"The mine ghost, the gnomes and mountain goblins, the dwarfs…the good and evil spirits, the demons and devils played an important role in the history of mining," said mining author Wolfgang Paul.

Entities of former miners and other lingering human presences were equally abundant in the diggings. Ghosts of many types drifted along the tunnels—dead or lost miners and women, of whom most diggers had a mortal fear when they entered the mines. With the exception of females, alive or otherwise, the undead that haunted the workings were generally not cause for alarm, said one Gunnison County miner's aphorism that appeared in an 1889 issue of the White Pine Cone.

"Ghosts in a mine can work no evil, but 'spirits' below play the devil."

Other "ghosts" prowling the workings included the fired worker who returned to unnerve mine owners, the hired ghosts sent by one company to a competitor's mine to make mischief, and the pranksters who created ghosts for fun.

Every experienced miner easily could tell the difference between aboveground and subterranean phantoms by their appearance or the noises they produced.

"Surface ghosts shriek and gibber and wail and moan. Underground ghosts knock and creak, and jingle the steel," said Fisher Vane in 1937. "Above-ground ghosts, from a compilation of memories are usually whole ones. Down in the deeps they've been known to stroll through the workings minus arms, legs, and even heads."

Cold, calculating and thoroughly scientific, the mining engineers said the apparitions were merely dancing shadows thrown on walls by flickering candles, and unexplained noises only the sound of rock settling on timbers following shots. Vane, on the other hand, echoed the sentiments of the wizened men who hammered steel into rock in near darkness beneath the earth.

"Your dyed-in-the-jeans hardrock miner, though, knows better—t'hell with thim yeller-legged ingineers! What the heck do they know about underground ghosts?"

Underground Apparitions

"We have a real thoroughbred ghost over at North Fork. His ghostship holds forth at the May Mazeppa Mine and has succeeded in turning several heads of hair a beautiful gray. He, she, or it, wears a regulation graveyard shroud and with a pick stalks barefoot through the gloomy galleries of tunnel Number 4, stopping suddenly at a miner's side to extinguish his candle by a single breath and paralyze the miner with terror."

—*White Pine Cone*, November 1887

* * * * * * *

GHOSTLY GRIT FROM THE MORNING STAR

During the late summer of 1879, a traveler from Leadville wandered into the office of the Daily Reporter Call in Central City with an unearthly tale that transpired in the depths of the Morning Star Mine in Leadville's Strayhorse Gulch.

Several days earlier, he told the news reporter, a man died in one of the drifts of that mine when he was buried by tons of falling rock. As a result, none of the miners would work in the place where their luckless companion perished, fearing a post-mortem visit from the man's wandering shade. The day after the accident, an unsuspecting German immigrant arrived looking for work. He was hired immediately and sent into the drift where his predecessor met his demise. Unaware of what previously transpired in the mine, the new man rode to the bottom of the shaft and climbed off the bucket. Immediately, he began to shake the hoist rope violently, a signal to those on the surface that something was amiss.

When the men above called down in response, the German said there was a dead man in the drift. He apparently stumbled across the body in the pale candlelight and surmised that someone fell down the shaft during the night. The hoistman told him to put the corpse in the bucket, and when the grim task was done, the new employee signaled to the men at the windlass to begin raising the mangled cargo to the surface. When the bucket emerged from the ground, it was empty.

At lunchtime, the German came up and demanded an explanation, thinking that the other miners were playing pranks on him. When told the bucket came up without the dead man, he insisted that he put the body in it as instructed. Not knowing anyone had died in the mine, the German was able to give the exact description and appearance of the miner whose body he placed in the bucket. It matched that of the man who was killed there. After his uncanny experience and hearing the details of the accident, the new man also refused to work in that portion of the mine.

* * * * * * *

"Last Sunday night, about twelve o'clock, the engineer of the Golden colliery was alone hoisting water. When the cage came up, he asserts that the ghost of Johnny Wearne, the murdered engineer, was sitting on the top! The first time he let him back into the shaft, but when he came back the second time, he dropped everything and ran, without reversing the engine. As a consequence, the cage was run to the top of the derrick, and things pretty badly smashed."

—Colorado Springs Gazette, December 12, 1874

These massive iron boulders along Toledo Avenue mark the caved entrance of the California and Colorado Tunnel. In 1886, ghostly mayhem from inside the abandoned mine made sleep difficult for nearby neighbors, at least until one resident finally summoned police to quell the racket. O'Malley arrived, and in true ghostly form, the rowdy spirits stopped the clamor and remained quiet until the man in blue was gone.

'FIENDISH PANDEMONIUM'

One hundred yards south of the Bohn Mine, where Toledo Avenue leaves the Leadville City Limits, the historic California Gulch Road passes an aspen grove containing the ruins of a residence from another era. Just beyond, several enormous black boulders strewn here and there among the sagebrush along the left side of the route mark the site of the long-collapsed portal of the California and Colorado Tunnel.

Located in May 1879, the mine pierced Carbonate Hill for a distance of 1,100 ft. and produced gold, silver and lead ore that was hauled to daylight through the seven-foot by seven-foot adit. That year, 475 feet into the hill, miners blasted their way into a "bonanza pocket" of chlorides that assayed 16,357 ounces of silver per ton of ore. During the early days of the mining camp, the tunnel was the scene of property disputes and numerous accidents.

By 1880, the mine was abandoned but residents living near the entrance to the tunnel were tormented by the clatter of phantom miners working every night inside the bore. By day, local children patted mud into pies in the stream of water that flowed from the opening, until one summer evening when an apparition from beyond the veil strode up, scared them away and put an end to their youthful entertainment.

So annoying was the midnight racket that one neighborhood woman finally laid down the law. She went to the police, saying that a "fiendish pandemonium" was going on all through the night at the tunnel. An obliging officer accompanied her to the spot and finding nothing unusual, he returned to his beat on Harrison Avenue.

Passing near the portal of the mine, many urbanites said they saw the apparition of an ex-gulch resident from bygone days. Sporting a ragged beard and dark facial spots that disappeared by his neck, some said it was the spirit of "Billy the Woodchopper", who died years earlier on the gilded banks California Gulch.

During his mortal tenure in the gully, Billy was a 35-year old eccentric who managed to attract an audience wherever he went.

One warm August afternoon, to the horror of the watchers, he set sail for the celestial regions as they looked on. With a bucket of water in each hand and one-half dozen pairs of eyes following him, Bill was making his way down the hill below the Coronel Sellers Mine when blood began streaming from his mouth. He fell, and in moments 12 hands tenderly carried him to the Oro Saloon, where he died without uttering a word. Since no one knew his real name, Billy was committed to the ground at Evergreen without the appropriate obsequies.

As a result, Bill's nocturnal high jinks at the tunnel created a local sensation. Many Leadville residents visited the deserted mine after sundown to hear the ghostly racket and hopefully catch a glimpse of the nameless phantom for themselves.

Even as Billy was clattering around the drifts in the C&C Tunnel, another phantasm, distraught over his dire demise beneath Long and Derry Hill, was stalking the dismal galleries of the Fortuna Tunnel.

* * * * * * *

"A veritable ghost is reported to be playing sorry tricks on the miners of Ute Creek in Clear Creek County. It drives miners out of their cabins at night, and plays havoc with their little furniture. Neither stones nor bullets affect him."

—*White Pine Cone, May 15, 1885*

* * * * * * *

- Fortuna Tunnel

"Fred T. Robinson re-opened the old Fortuna and began hauling ore from the upper tunnel. There may be ghosts around the mine, but Mr. R can stand a few as long as he has big bodies of ore and more to come."

—*Breckenridge Bulletin, June 12, 1901*

LOST HIS HEAD BUT DIDN'T STAY DEAD

In October 1894, an old prospector was quoted as being skeptical of all things supernatural underground.

"Some of the miners claim to have seen ghosts around the old shafts," he observed. "Well, that's all right. It makes good stuff for the newspapers to talk about—but let me tell you, young man, there are no ghosts around these mines. I've been mining for thirty years and have seen men killed and mangled and have been in old shafts a hundred times but never have I heard of the spook or have seen a man who claimed to have seen one."

Apparently, for all his experience, the gentleman never ventured onto Long and Derry Hill to brave an encounter with the horrible specter haunting the carbonate-encrusted galleries of the Fortuna Tunnel. Tales of unearthly activity there churned their way through Iowa Gulch mining circles in the 1880s following a ghastly slaying that occurred in the mine.

"This spot had always been regarded with more or less distrust by many prospectors," said a Leadville daily in 1900. "The shadow of a tragedy hung over it, and no one had any desire to hunt for ore in a place that had been cursed with a murder. It was an unlucky spot, so the general superstition went…with gruesome stories of moving lights and ghostly forms in the vicinity of the old workings."

It was no accident that claimed the life of Philemon Marsh at the tunnel that sunny Sunday morning in 1885. Once inside, he met fellow miner Henry Kidder to do some work, but things turned sour when the two began to quarrel while calculating a distance. They disagreed about using the tunnel in order to work the Houston claim, part of which cut across the Fortuna. Kidder asked Marsh to hold one end of a measuring tape, and at the same time muttered something about not wanting him in the diggings. Marsh, ever ready for an argument, promptly told him to go to the Devil.

Not to be outdone, Kidder wasted no time picking up the axe leaning against a timber and striking his partner in the neck, almost completely severing head from body. A pair of miners working nearby, one of whom narrowly missed being sprayed by the fountain of blood, witnessed the murder. High-tailing it from the tunnel, one of them ran across Rock Hill to the Crown Point Mine, where he telephoned the sheriff of the troubling news.

When the constable and the coroner drove up, the pair followed the red-tinted stream that led into the tunnel and found Marsh between the tracks in the embrace of death, his head lying in a pool of blood and water. A thin strand of neck muscle was the only thing holding it to the body. Later, at the morgue, crowds of people lined up outside the office to view the remains and see the result of an axe stroke that left a hole in the victim's neck big enough to hold a grapefruit.

Marsh, a quarrelsome man with a mean disposition, was unmarried and came to Leadville from Pennsylvania. Kidder, known to be calm and without fear, was not considered the dangerous sort, unless of course you were the one holding the other end of the tape measure.

Death didn't always signal the end of a relationship, especially when strong emotions were involved, and Marsh carried the most intense distress with him on his journey from Iowa Gulch to the Pearly Gates.

While shifts at the Fortuna were a lot quieter without the abusive and foul-tempered Keystoner on hand to stir things up, the axe-man wasn't so fortunate. After being detained by the sheriff for the killing, Kidder eventually returned to his duties at the Fortuna. Marsh's nearly headless apparition wasted no time confronting his assassin as he mucked out the corner of a drift. The murdered miner wasn't in a good mood, especially after being put on display like a pork chop in a Leadville butcher shop. Apparently, beheading didn't affect the phantom's vocal chords, and Marsh promptly launched into an earful of otherworldly invective that would curl a miner's whiskers. He told Kidder he would see him again and get his revenge.

Underground Apparitions

–Carbonate Chronicle, May 13, 1901

Like the Grim Reaper gathering his macabre harvest, Henry Kidder lopped off the head of an offensive co-worker with one well-aimed axe stroke, dispatching him to a troubled post-mortem existence and unleashing a series of otherworldly affairs that ended with the untimely demise of the murderer.

* * * * * * *

Kidder, a skeptic concerning things supernatural, passed off the experience to lack of sleep and nightmares following the affair inside the Fortuna. A year passed with no sign of the phantom, and it wasn't until August 1886 that the one-rime miner and his murderer met again near the spot where the decapitation occurred.

Underground Apparitions

    Kidder was the last in line of a group of day-shift miners making their way out of the mountain at quitting time. Fifty yards from the entrance, the ghost of Marsh materialized. Barely visible from where it stood beneath a set of timbers, the spirit cursed and again uttered its threat before dissolving into the half-light. The sight of the apparition and a reddish tint to the groundwater that trickled from the tunnel's mouth made a dire impression and Kidder quit the Fortuna. He found work two gulches to the north in the Maid of Erin Mine on the north slope of Carbonate Hill.

- Maid of Erin Mine around 1900

Fortune's Wheel deemed that Henry Kidder's doom would be sealed during an elevator ride in the Maid of Erin Shaft in 1888. Witnesses to the accident said a mysterious passenger was responsible for his ghastly demise.
Denver Public Library Western History Collection, X-60968

* * * * * * *

    Miners at the Maid, at least those who never heard about the measuring incident over in Iowa Gulch, described Kidder as a good-natured man. But at age 30, the dice of destiny delivered him a horrendous fate one day during the summer of 1888.
    Boarding one of the side-by-side elevators in the shaft, Kidder and a pair of companions headed for the surface following a day of drilling, mucking and blasting in an ore zone beneath Strayhorse Gulch. The three men rode in silence until, without

warning, Kidder appeared to stumble to one side of the cage, his body lurching against the elevator door and his head tipping over the top of the shoulder-high gate. In a split second, that portion of his anatomy was caught and crushed by the bottom of the cage descending in the adjoining shaft compartment.

Later, his corpse also was placed on public display at the undertaker's, this time as an example of the mortician's skill. The embalmer used several boxes of plaster of Paris to build up the crushed bones of the skull.

"So cleverly has the work been done that a close inspection will scarcely show that the head had been injured at all," said the newspaper the day after the accident.

Kidder's body was sent to the family home in the Midwest. Following the incident, the doomed man's companions recalled one thing most curious about the elevator ride on that fateful day. Both said they momentarily saw the figure of a fourth man in the cage and heard the apparition utter an epithet before shoving Kidder against the elevator door.

* * * * * * *

"Some of the miners on Fletcher Mountain have been badly frightened by a 'ghost' that has made its unwelcome appearance in their cabin so that no one of them will occupy the cabin alone. They hear, or think they hear, strange noises at night, and see ghostly specters gliding about the room. Their clothes are scattered over the floor by some unknown hand, and various other tricks are played by this supposed visitor from the netherworld. They thought some of deserting the place altogether, but they were making money, and concluded to stay; but none of them will sleep in that cabin alone."

—*Leadville Daily Herald*, September 25, 1884

- First National Mine

Would the Bedlam created by Fred Carlson's spectral persecutors or only the sound of dripping water greet the ears of an attentive listener at the collar of the abandoned First National Shaft?

FRED'S FIRST NATIONAL GRIEVANCE

Across Iowa Gulch and a little west of the Fortuna Tunnel stands the weathered headframe of the First National Mine, where Fred Carlson once shoveled and blasted ore for the company. Being a diligent worker, he didn't like to be bothered while engaged in a task. In fact, he took his work so seriously that in the spring of 1899, his companions began to wonder if he hadn't been underground too long or if the powder fumes hadn't gone to his head. It was then that someone anonymously notified the sheriff, saying that Carlson had finally lost his candle wax.

Carlson and his partner were at work in an ordinary drift 150 ft. underground when the miner began to complain of ghosts. The vaporous visitors peered over his shoulder, he said, seeped in and out of his coat sleeves, tickled his earlobes and got downright bossy when it came to timbering. Like so many swarming insects, phantoms infiltrated drilling operations, pestered him while he handled dynamite and made mucking miserable.

Generally not given to complaining, Carlson began to grumble about the large gathering of spooks that made their rendezvous everywhere he went, "flitting about him incessantly and keeping him from his work", said a Leadville newspaper report.

One Thursday evening Carlson had enough. Swatting and threatening brought no relief, but only served to intensify the torment. He came to the surface for supper, finished his pickled herring and cheese on hard tack and immediately began looking for a gun he could use to drive his impalpable persecutors from the mine. When he didn't find one, he threatened to lob a smoldering stick or two of giant powder at his tormenters.

Arriving at the First National none too soon, Sheriff Kennedy stepped from the bucket onto the first level and found Fred grumbling about the spook that just stole his hammer and crimping a cap on the charge he would use to send his hecklers into oblivion once and for all. The lawman deliberated with Carlson about the unearthly torment and convinced him to forget the dynamite, come to town and swear out warrants for the spectral revelers. Carlson agreed and walked the three miles to Leadville to file the complaints, but instead was taken into jail until his sanity could be evaluated.

- "Mines on Fryer Hill "(The Illustrated London News)
Labyrinthine diggings beneath Fryer Hill were plagued by otherworldly visitations. Even the one-half ton of candles used in Leadville's mines every day during the summer of 1878 wasn't enough to keep restless spirits at bay. By 1884, ghosts in the Chrysolite Mine could wail their way through nine miles of underground workings.

* * * * * * *

"Empire is enjoying a sensation in the shape of a ghost which regularly visits one of the mines and goes howling through the drifts and tunnels."
—White Pine Cone, February 12, 1886

* * * * * * *

Underground Apparitions

THE PENROSE GHOST

>An old prospector stood on Penrose dump,
>And in his hand he held a lump
>Of ore that came from the Penrose claim;
>'Lead Carbonates' was this ore's name,
>That once brought Leadville note and fame;
>But he laid it down, and with a sigh
>He said, "Old Leadville's dead; she must die;"
>The pumps had stopped, was the reason why.
>But long, long hence
>The old prospector lies out by the fence,
>And the pumps are running this very day,
>While his bones commingle with the clay,
>But he thought he heard a whirring noise,
>And came down from above to see the boys,
>And his spirit gave an awful "Ah!"
>As he saw the water run down the draw,
>"I sure called that turn wrong," he said.
>"Old Leadville lives, and I am dead."

>(By 'Punks' Powers, Poet Laureate of the Penrose Crew.)
>*Carbonate Chronicle,* Oct. 4, 1915

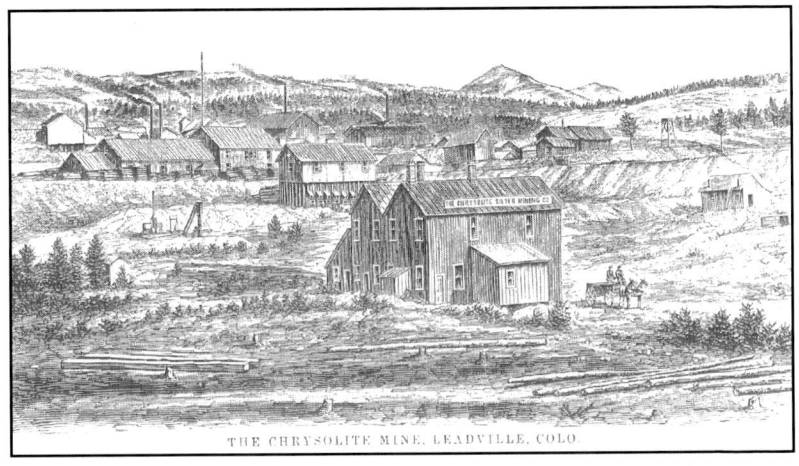

- Chrysolite Mine

The Roberts Shaft of the Chrysolite was the death site of William Moon, who joined the graveyard shift there in 1882 after he was impaled by a falling pipe while working at the bottom of the main shaft.

Illutstration courtesy of Robert Elder

MISSED HOLE AT THE MOYER

During the first decade of Leadville's existence, rich carbonate ore was mined from relatively shallow deposits located beneath the hills east of town. By 1890, the district's wealth was supposed to be exhausted, but a new era began with the location of a sulfide ore zone underlying the carbonates. Thus started the period of deep mining in the Plutonian regions under Iron and Breece hills. Spectral goings-on seemed to follow the ebb and flow of the mining industry.

One of the first ghosts to reside in the Leadville mines pestered laborers in the murky recesses of the New Discovery Lode in 1878. Miners reported that a phantom woman, dressed in a grave shroud, haunted the workings deep under Fryer Hill. A handful of courageous men attempted to catch the banshee, intent on hauling her to the surface in the bucket and exorcising her from the workings, but the attempted eviction was in vain. When they managed to get close to the ghoul, she floated out of reach and down the drift, turning to spit fire before vanishing into the blackness.

As if to protest the intrusion into their dark, silent digs, ghosts generally faded from the workings during times of peak mining activity, only to return when the fever of the silver boom began to wane. As Leadville celebrated its second decade, the epicenter of ghostly doings filtered deep into the diggings beneath Iron Hill.

Located in California Gulch, two miles southeast of the Leadville City Limits, the Moyer Mine lies adjacent to County Road 2, near the point where the Mineral Belt Trail crosses the gulch between Iron and Rock hills.

At the turn of the 20th Century, the Moyer was among the premier lodes in California Gulch. Its engine room had a double-drum hoist with a gauge showing the exact location of the cage or bucket in the shaft. In an adjacent building were four large boilers and the largest air compressor in the Leadville area. The Moyer Shaft had three compartments: one for the elevator, another for buckets and the third, a manway, containing piping and ladders.

Underground Apparitions

In 1904, the Moyer produced an average of 11,000 tons per month of low-grade zinc sulphide and was the largest producer of such ore in the state. In 1917, when the mine closed after decades of production, workers were laid off but a skeleton crew of ethereal tunnelers stayed on.

–Coronel Sellers & Moyer mines-1885
Near the downstream end of Oro City, the Coronel Sellers and Moyer mines produced zinc sulfide, lead carbonate and dead men, but spectral visitors preferred to frequent the Moyer's dismal workings rather than the wet, unstable stopes of the Sellers. This 1885 Photo shows three of the four Sellers shafts on the south slope of Iron Hill, the A.Y/Minnie Mine and the ghost-infested Moyer at the right.
–Denver Public Library Western History Collection, Aulls & Cannon, X-60970

* * * * * * *

By the turn of the century, stories of ghosts in the Moyer workings were common, particularly after one unfortunate accident there in 1901.

State Senator Joseph Gallagher came to Leadville from Silver Plume and took a job at the Moyer in January of that year. His employment ended abruptly two weeks later while at work in a drift when he went to look at an unexploded hole and was blown into the next life. Soon afterward, miners reported seeing the senator's ghost, pick over his shoulder, wandering the property and moaning "Beware!" Often descending the shaft in the bucket to warn his friends of danger, his specter seemed to melt into the workings, never returning to the surface.

Jonnie Cumfrey was a trammer who saw Gallagher's shade while pushing a loaded ore car along a third-level drift toward the shaft. Working reluctantly near the spot where the senator was smitten with death, he felt the car come to a stop as if being held back by some unseen force. Cumfrey looked up to see what the problem was and was greeted by the mutilated visage of the dead senator with arms outstretched. Knowing that apparitions frequently were omens that an accident was about to occur, Cumfrey listened to his intuition as he watched the gory phantom dissolve into the darkness. He left the loaded car with the ex-senator's ghost, ran from the drift and frantically rang for the bucket. Once on the surface, he collected his pay but after several days at home listening to the taunts of his companions, he relented to the abuse and returned to work. Cumfrey should have heeded the dead man's warning and stayed away because the day he returned to the Moyer, he fell into a chute and fractured a leg.

Gallagher's shade was at home both above and below ground. When not roaming the diggings beneath the gulch, miners having dinner on the surface often reported seeing the headless apparition of the former politician descending the north slope of Rock Hill, grub bucket in one hand and his head securely tucked under the other arm.

Today, the surface structures of the Moyer are gone and only red bricks, lead-colored cinders and a few slabs of fractured concrete mark the site of the haunted mine. Even the gaping shaft that once greeted curious travelers who stopped to peer down and drop a stone into the inky depths was capped in recent years to prevent accidents. There really was no need for such drastic safety measures—Senator Gallagher's benevolent ghost still roams the surface and underground workings of the great zinc producer, warning his vaporous colleagues and modern-day visitors of danger.

* * * * * * *

Underground Apparitions

- Mikado Mine-1920
Ghosts in the Mikado were almost as abundant as the silver bars produced at the mine.
Denver Public Library Western History Collection, X-61222

MR. GALLAGHER'S GHOST

One of the greatest Leadville mines, located at the northern end of Graham Park, also was deeply shrouded in the supernatural. For more than a century, the district's most eerie legend has been floating on the wind and moaning around the shaft house of the Mikado Mine. The story involves a pair of mining properties, four men named Gallagher, a plot to get rid of a mine boss and death in its most hideous forms.

Located by a trio of penniless Irish brothers named Gallagher in 1876, their lucky strike had an arboreal connection. A common version of the discovery tells how one of the brothers, on his way home from an all-night spree in an Oro City public house, tripped over an exposed pine root. His boot pried up a rock, which somehow was launched into the air, rebounding off his head. Cursing, he slipped the offending stone into his pocket for later disposal in the nearest abandoned shaft. At breakfast the next day, his brothers noticed the knot on the man's head and asked if he had a set-to in the saloon. Producing the stone and explaining how it came into his possession, the trio determined the accident was probably the work of some benevolent mountain sprite and decided to return to the spot and stake a claim.

Another version of the story tells how the brothers asked their former employer, "Uncle Billy" Stevens where to dig for silver. He reportedly took them to a vantage point on Iron Hill and dispatched them in the direction a large tree in Strayhorse Gulch. There they dug and found rich ore at a depth of 15 feet.

They called their discovery the Gallagher, or Camp Bird Mine, and it did well until 1883 when production began to wane. As the whims of fortune would have it, a new ore body was located one soggy day when the wheels of a heavily loaded wagon sank deep into the spring mud and rotated up rich mineral from a zone that would later produce $100,000. The property was reorganized in 1887 and christened the Mikado, employing 120 men.

Two years later, the Mikado was pouring out $200,000 in silver a month, including one 100-ton lot that brought $56,000. "Bonanza pockets" of ore, containing almost pure silver chloride were common in the mine and so rich that their contents were removed, placed in sacks and locked in the office strongbox for safekeeping. Once they got wind of the rich discoveries, local ore thieves began hatching plans to waylay ore wagons traveling between the mine and smelter. As a result, the Mikado became the only mine in the Leadville District to produce and ship solid silver bars.

Once their dreams were realized, the Gallaghers sold the mine for $250,000 and embarked on a world tour. Meanwhile, the Mikado continued to smile on its new owners.

"The stories concerning the riches of the Mikado sound like fairy tales," said the Leadville Daily & Evening Chronicle in 1889. "The marvelous performance of the early bonanza mines are being discounted by the Mikado, which is today, beyond all reasonable doubt, the richest silver mine in the world."

Not only was the mine rich, it was thoroughly haunted and well known for its resident ghost population until after 1900. Today, little remains of the history behind the legends.

"As kids, everyone was afraid of Gallagher's Ghost," said life-long Leadville resident Carl Miller. "Nobody even knew where the mine was, but when we were out playing 'kick-the-can' and we didn't want to come in, our parents would tell us Gallagher's Ghost or the Lady in Black would get us."

Miller's grandmother lived at 402 East Fourth Street, below the imposing Penrose Mine, which once stood castle-like and forbidding on the northern brow of Chicken Hill. It was a convenient, in-town place for youngsters to go to get scared. However, legends concerning the Gallagher Ghost were born one mile to the east in the mines of Strayhorse Gulch, where the workings of the old Argentine Mining Company perforate the south side of the gully.

Many fatalities were recorded at the Mikado, and at least eight miners boarded the Stygian Ferry there in the waning years of the 20th Century, five within a span of six months. Three walked into open shafts with fatal results, three more fell from buckets, one plunged into perdition from a ladder and another perished in a cave-in.

Underground Apparitions

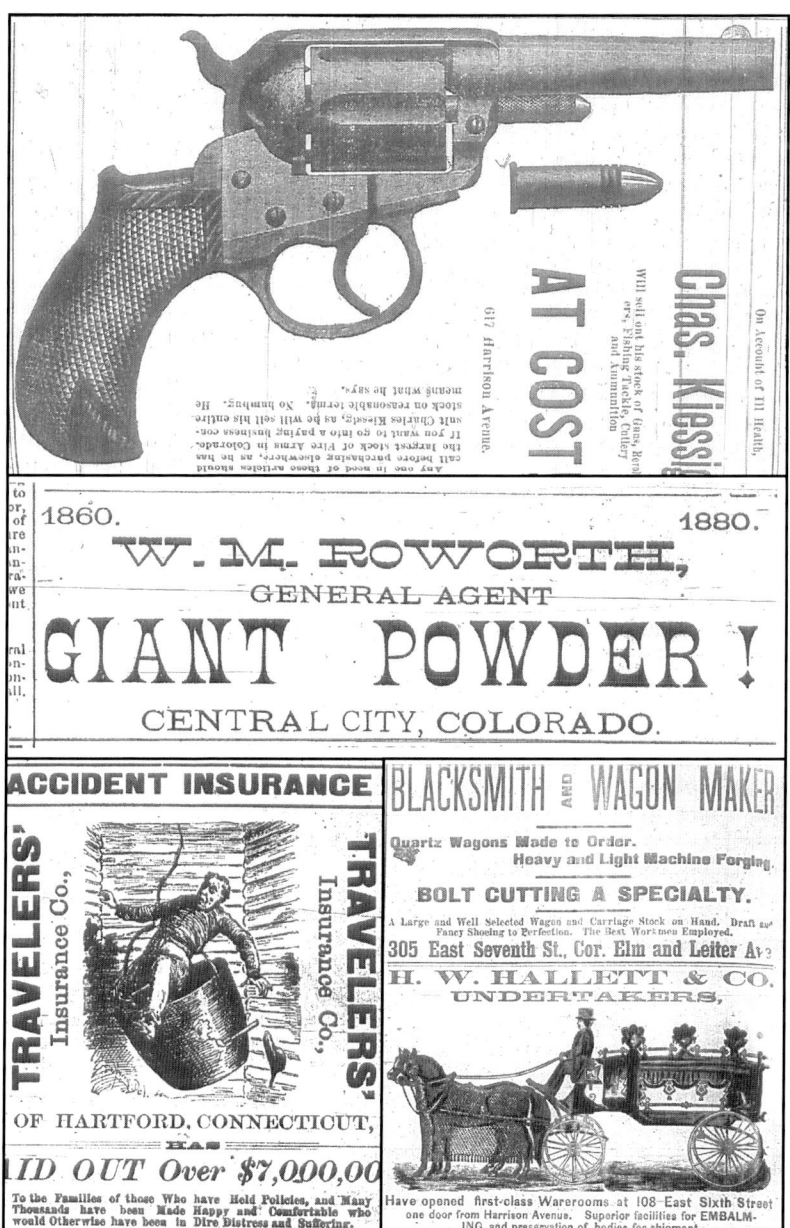

Purveyors of giant powder, pistols and insurance policies were well aware of the need for all three in the mining camps. The Leadville Undertaking Company often took charge of the results of explosions, gunfire and other fatal mishaps.

Underground Apparitions

James Slattery was the sixth miner to meet destruction at the Mikado or "Hole in the Wall Mine", when he was crushed by a falling slab of porphyry in 1898. A year later, Faulk died in a dizzying drop from a ladder, and Brown, an old miner who never carried matches, walked into a winze and traveled 40 ft. to the next world. Five of the dead men, including Slattery, Faulk, Brown and two others reportedly returned in spirit form to roam the workings of the Mikado, putting in their posthumous appearance at least once a month.

"A veritable spook who wanders about the shafts and levels ambles with the recklessness of a shadow through the machinery of the hoisting plant and skips lightly from surface to lowest depths as caprice or necessity impels him," a 1900 issue of the Denver Times said of the haunting.

For 10 years after Slattery's death, stories of strange beings hovering in the workings floated everywhere in the Mikado's dark, damp depths. The phantom quintet reportedly jumped unexpectedly onto moving ore cars, murmured and moaned with disembodied voices, placed invisible icy hands on shoulders or appeared as a gossamer veil floating through the drift. Working on all levels of the mine, spooks were the reason buckets wouldn't move, cages rattled for no reason and signal bells rang with no one around to pull the cord. Miners agreed there was genuine otherworldly business at work in the Mikado, and according to the Leadville Evening Chronicle of the day, the supernatural events that followed the deaths resulted in workers quitting and demanding their pay. Many took jobs in mines with less spiritual unrest.

Men riding the elevator to and from their worksite reported seeing the form of an otherworldly miner standing at the opening of the abandoned second level. Beckoning for the bucket to stop, he also was known to pull the bell signal rope. So frequently was the apparition seen that the mine manager undertook an investigation. Inspectors descended to the second-level station and there saw the ghost standing near the entrance of the drift.

"The men stepped into the level, and this ghostly guide could be seen, receding into the blackness. He was followed for a considerable distance, moving slowly ahead, through the old drifts and cross-cuts, and finally disappeared into a winze," reported the Aspen Tribune.

The searchers abandoned the effort after inspecting the winze and finding nothing.

"There was something weird, something beyond the mind of man," said the Leadville press about the unearthly occurrences in the mine. "Many miners have come to the conclusion that they are the wailings of men who have lost their lives in the mines."

One company superintendent in 1889 said, "I am somewhat inclined to believe in the thing, for many of our men whom I have accounted extremely sound mentally, have quit their work at the most unusual hours and demanded their 'time', saying they would not go down the shaft again for thousands of dollars."

Not only did he say the mine was haunted, the superintendent also believed there to be a curse upon the place and that it would be unsafe for any man to attempt to fight the mysterious and unholy power controlling the property.

Some workers weren't so quick to look for work elsewhere, but regarded the resident spooks in a favorable light.

These miners, said a Leadville daily, "…are men whom the devil couldn't scare and they proceed with their work singing and repeating the words of all the ballads at their command."

They became accustomed to the presence of their shadowy companions, saying that the spirits were not generally harmful, but sometimes mischievous. Their real mission, said an edition of the Denver Times, was to act as guardians of the men working in the dangerous drifts.

Besides betting on the good intentions of their invisible companions, miners relied on their own cabalistic practices to ward off the Grim Reaper's call by invoking the protection of charms and rituals. One miner from Cornwall went through the same routine every day. As he boarded the bucket to be lowered into the Mikado shaft, he took a piece of blue chalk from his coat and sketched a cross on a piece of slate that hung on a nearby post. After drawing a circle around the cross, he placed the chalk in his pocket and gave a nod to the hoistman to lower the bucket.

Underground Apparitions

So convinced was this miner of the protective qualities of the rite that he never failed to practice it, especially at his spook-ridden Leadville worksite.

- Unidentified Leadville mine- 1880

Whether toiling underground or on the surface, death always looked over the miner's shoulder, and accidents purged the ranks of underground workers with grim regularity. Miners generally refused to work in a place where someone died, thus avoiding the risk of a chance encounter with visitors from beyond the grave. Denver Public Library Western History Collection, #10060879

* * * * * * *

On one occasion, while working in the tin mines of Cornwall, he didn't perform the ceremony and was the victim of an accident in which he suffered a broken arm. After immigrating to America, he continued the practice, but was so ridiculed by his American colleagues that one morning he didn't carry out the formality. The same day, he was injured in an explosion that cost him two fingers.

Several Mikado diggers scoffed at the unexplained events that were so common at the worksite, saying they were the work of a practical joker. On one occasion they ran to the spot where they heard the unearthly noises, arriving with pistols drawn but finding nothing. Another workman was stricken with fear when he saw the shade of a miner wearing ragged brown overalls, slouch hat and blue spectacles. He plunged his shovel through the misty form, which promptly vanished in the lurid candlelight.

At least some of the unexplained activity in the mine was attributed to pranks authored by stockholders intent on getting rid of mine manager W. R. Chadbourne, a firm believer in spiritualism. The investors weren't happy that the boss preferred to sink profits back into the mine rather than return dividends to them. They endeavored to capitalize on the ghost mania by convincing miners to engrave spooky figures on beams, fill the grooves with powder or phosphorus and ignite them, creating glowing images of a sulfurous man in areas the manager was known to frequent. Tricksters also produced ghostly voices, floating candles and mutilated bodies in drifts in order to scare Chadbourne from the mine. The charades didn't work but instead frightened numerous workers into collecting their paychecks.

Despite manufactured efforts to run the superintendent out of the Mikado, other uncanny events pointed to unexplainable and seemingly supernatural powers at work. The Mikado crew identified the voices of two of the spectral miners. Before their deaths, Chadbourne ordered the pair to report to work in a particularly dangerous area of the mine known as the Black Stope. The men reluctantly followed orders and as they walked into the darkness toward the hazardous cavern, one of them turned and said that if he died there, he would return to haunt the manager. Both were killed and in the days following the accident, as Chadbourne walked alone underground one afternoon, an unseen hand fell on his shoulder and a voice proclaimed, "Well, Chad, I told you I would haunt you, and here I am."

* * * * * * *

Underground Apparitions

Mine superintendent W.R. Chadbourne stepped on the stockholders toes and became the victim of counterfeit spooks, even as the genuine article hobnailed it through the workings.

* * * * * * *

"There is an unearthly presence in the underground workings and the thought of meeting this strange spirit, apparently clothed in fleshly garments, is more than some of the stoutest hearts can entertain with equanimity," said an April 1900 issue of the Aspen Tribune.

Many Mikado miners firmly believed that the ghosts haunting the mine were those of the men killed there, watching over them and warning them of danger. One was a flesh and bone employee named Cyrus, who was drilling the face of a drift near an upraise when he heard a frantic voice calling from below, "Oh, Cy, come down here quick!"

Thinking something serious was happening, he scrambled to the bottom of the winze. When he arrived, he found no one there but heard the sound of fifty tons of boulders falling onto the spot where he was hammering only moments before.

Ghosts in the Mikado not only served as guardians but also tormented their living counterparts by ringing signal bells after everyone was raised to the surface. Each time they did, the entire mine had to be searched before the hoist was shut down for the night. At the end of each futile hunt, the sound of maniacal laughter told the explorers that ghosts were responsible for the prank.

Many miners reported hearing hollow-sounding voices saying "Hello!" as they walked along the mine's deserted drifts. When a chorus of two-dozen human voices in all parts of the Mikado responded with "Hello!" everyone knew the dead had returned once again to occupy the drifts. During times when the mine was not in operation, pedestrians on the road below the shaft house often heard the sounds of picks, shovels and groaning voices emanating from the depths of the shaft.

"The men are not frightened," the Times continued, "but when it is suggested that they are victims of their own imagination, the only reply is a look that is more eloquent than words."

None of the original brothers Gallagher of Mikado fame were believed to be the ones who returned to the mine in ghostly form. Instead, that honor was bestowed upon the Silver Plume senator whose head was blown to atoms in the Moyer in 1901.

Completing the tale was the haunted venue of the Mikado, or "Gallagher Mine", which provided the grim body count and ghost-ridden underground workings. The resulting blend of the eerie history of two mines and the same name connected to both gives Leadville the legendary spectral cocktail known today as "Gallagher's Ghost".

* * * * * * *

"'Buzz' Howe is down from Silverton. Buzz said Slattery was the ghost."
—*Durango Democrat*, June 2, 1907

* * * * * * *

CHAPTER EIGHT
URBAN HAUNTS

* * * * * *

"Ghosts did shriek and squeal about the streets"

— William Shakespeare, Julius Caesar

* * * * * *

LEADVILLE'S HAUNTED HILL

By 1883, the Leadville populace was accustomed to ghosts wandering at large, following years of alleged visitations from beyond the grave. Derelict and forlorn cabins in the vicinity had a long history of being infested by spooks, and for the residents of Capitol Hill, an abandoned homestead at 500 West Eighth Street became the scene of nightly apparitions.

Standing vacant among the stumps of harvested timber, no one dared approach the haunted house, even in the light of day. After nightfall, ghostly visitations occurred with such regularity that neighbors were glued to the windowpanes of their homes in hopes of catching a glimpse of the phantoms that made their nightly rendezvous there.

At precisely 10 p.m., as neighbors behind glass looked on with chattering teeth, a female ghost materialized out of the gloom and disappeared through the doorway of the structure. Soon, the indistinct shade of a man appeared, walking around the tree stumps before passing through the door of the abandoned house. Sometimes, the woman wore an elegant white dress and at other times sported more common attire. Occasionally, the couple was observed lingering together among the truncated pine stumps before retreating to the interior of the dwelling.

Urban Haunts

A GOOD INDICATION.

- Victorian couple, Scribner's Monthly
One pair of Leadville lovebirds discovered that a forlorn and allegedly haunted cabin offered the seclusion they needed to carry on an intrigue that was impossible by the light of day.

* * * * * * *

One evening, a stalwart neighborhood resident walked across the hill, concealed himself and waited for the phantoms to arrive. At the designated hour, the mysterious woman walked out of the darkness from the direction of Seventh Street and the male ghost drifted up from Harrison Avenue. Embracing, the phantom pair talked in hushed tones, apparently unaware they were being watched. They entered the cabin and remained there 30 minutes before leaving and walking toward the avenue. As the couple strolled by the spy, he noticed they were not astral beings, but thoroughly human, in fact, prominent socialites in the city who wisely chose a haunted house for the illicit rendezvous.

Not surprisingly, the nocturnal hilltop encounters stopped after the details of the 'haunting' appeared in a local newspaper the following day.

* * * * * * *

"Reports of a haunted house have reached the ears of the teacher at Iron Hill and she proposes to 'Lay the Ghost' by moving into the premises and speaking peace to Whiskey Tim's troubled soul."

--The Herald Democrat, October 28, 1900

* * * * * * *

CATCHING GHOSTS

"Ghostland must, in truth, be a realm of spicy variety and absolute independence," said a Carbonate Chronicle newsman during the fall of 1900 in an article that outlined the characteristics of phantasms. He detailed the appearance and substance of ghosts as documented by psychic researchers in more than 1,000 hauntings during the last decade of the 19th Century.

Gray was the prevailing color of apparitions, the writer said, while others appeared dressed in black. Many took on a luminous appearance, especially when encountered by the light of the moon.

"Modern specters differ quite as widely as to their substance," the scribe continued. "Many are vaporous and intangible. Others can be distinctly felt. Some are so heavy that they can weigh their victims down. Others are so filmy that objects can pass through them…Then again, there are phantoms which take forms other than human."

Some specters were perceived as a misty pillar coming down a lane, a cloud emerging from the forest or balls of light in the darkness of a bedroom.

People haunted by ghosts reported feeling a variety of

sensations while touching an apparition, including the feel of rough clothing, an icy hand, a flimsy drapery or a wave of chilly air. In one case, the spook lay down near a friend in bed and placed its frozen lips against her cheek.

"The majority of ghosts simply vanish like breath into the wind. Others make their exits through bolted doors, slamming them loudly. Many of these doors are seen to open, but later prove to be securely locked in the inside. Numerous spooks have a habit of vanishing as soon as spoken to."

* * * * * * *

"For some reason not easy to explain, the dead are supposed to be hostile to the living. Few people there be who would not run, terror-stricken, from a ghost."

—Oak Creek Times, November 3, 1910

* * * * * * *

'TOO GREEN TO BURN'

Even wandering souls of the dead looking for a good time found the wicked gaslight of State Street in 1880 a welcome place to spend eternity. Several of their frost-nipped number took up residence there with an upstanding Swedish family named Anderson during January of that year, plopping themselves down inside the carriage house located behind the residence. Before long, the frostbitten phantoms and their brazen behavior became the talk of the Lower State neighborhood.

Mr. Anderson first realized something wasn't right when he walked into the barn one winter evening and the axe he left sticking in a block of wood flew into the air, nearly cleaving his head on the way down. An examination of the tool and the block revealed nothing out of the ordinary so he split the evening's quota of fuel and returned to the house for supper. Over his coffee he mentioned the incident of the flying axe, and his daughter Annie said it was the work of ghosts that lived in the outbuilding. Both returned to the coach house and were greeted with the sound of knocking.

"It's the ghost," Annie announced. "They even answer questions."

Annie later told the newspaper reporter that one knock meant "yes" and a pair of raps, "no".

"The child seems to have made something of a study of the method of procedure adopted in the spirit world, for on Friday night she found out what the spirits wanted," the news article stated.

On the evening in question, father and daughter heard the sound of barrels rolling on the barn's wooden floor. Mining machinery was kept there, and peering through the window, the pair saw a 300-pound metal drum rolling back and forth under its own power. Mr. Anderson opened the door and the family cat, twice its normal size, sprang out and dashed into the safety of the house. The man asked Annie if she wanted to go in and see what he spirits wanted.

"Yes!" was her fearless reply.
Wrapped in the dim light within the carriage barn, a vigorous knocking sound emanated from the walls, floor and ceiling.

"What do you want?" asked the youngster.

Following the sound of three knocks, the axe again rose into the air and landed on a block of wood.

"Do you want kindling?" Annie inquired, at which one solid knock was heard.

Skeptically, Mr. Anderson went to the woodpile and soon had a neat pile of sticks ready for the stove. After he finished, the splitter flew into the chilly air and landed on a piece of coal. Annie said the ghosts had the cold shivers and wanted him to break up some coal into suitable size for igniting in a fire.

"Please hurry up so we can go in the house and get warm," the girl pleaded as her father smashed a few large chunks and threw the pieces into a box. Annie said the spirits wanted a fire built.

"The spirits can go to the devil if they want to get warm," Mr. Anderson said. "I'll not burn down my barn to please them."
At that moment, the axe rose into the air and stuck into a piece of wood.

"Why don't you assume some earthly form so I can knock the s— out of you?" he added.

"Just then such a cold draft of wind blew past that it almost froze him to the bone, and the axe lodged in the block of wood rose into the air, turned a double somersault, and came down within inches of Mr. Anderson's head," the newspaper reported. Annie said the refrigerated spirits needed to have a fire in the barn.

"What kind of hell are they in anyway, that they don't get roasted enough?" the elder Anderson said provocatively. "They must be too green to burn."

At that insult, the offended spirits began flinging coal and wood fast and thick inside the barn. Father and daughter fled into the frosty Leadville air and took refuge inside the house with the projectiles sailing after them. Lumps of coal and sticks continued to pelt the back of the residence until one stony missile shattered a windowpane.

Following the experience in the outbuilding, the Anderson household got no peace, and the family feline continued to display bizarre behavior. Annie suggested going to an aunt's house on East Fifth Street to spend the night.

"Mr. Anderson told her to bundle up darned quick and get out of the house with her infernal frozen spirits," the newspaper concluded.

After Annie's departure, the shivering specters shut the barn door and tranquility returned to the West State Street neighborhood. However, after a few days of peace and quiet, Mr. Anderson's curiosity over the affair led him to seek out a meeting of spiritualists. A medium advised him not to set fire to the barn, but to consider the possibility that the spirits therein wanted to convey a message.

One Saturday evening while Annie read _Owen's Footfalls on the Boundaries of Another World_, a misty shape condensed into the form of a boy who stood in the doorway of the kitchen. No one recognized the young man with the olive complexion and long, dark, curly hair as he stood barefoot and motionless staring back at the family through large brown eyes. The flames in the oil lamps scattered around the room changed from pale yellow to blue and a strange scent filled the room. Wearing a blue woolen coat and yellow pants, the specter simply turned his head, looked toward the door and pointed.

"He's my spirit guide," Annie announced, after which one solid knock sounded on the wall and the youthful apparition dissolved into thin air. Every evening after supper the ghost put in an appearance in the Anderson home, repeating the same mute ritual. The phenomenon aroused no shortage of interest in the city and since the phantasm never materialized during daylight hours, the family engaged a chemist to attempt to photograph the spirit in the lurid lamplight of the family kitchen.

AS COMFORTABLE AS CIRCUMSTANCES WILL ADMIT.

- Leadville couple at home, Scribner's Monthly

Otherworldly activity came to a dead stop when Annie took her frostbitten phantom friends to a sleepover at her aunt's house, leaving her mother and father at home to ponder the high mystery that possessed the carriage house.

* * * * * * *

Urban Haunts

"A survey of superstitions throughout the world discloses the fact that there are certain characteristics common to the ghosts of all nations. Among other things they suffer from hunger and cold. So the good-natured Breton peasant, when he goes to bed at night, is in the habit of leaving a little food on the table and some fire in the grate so that the poor ghosts may eat and warm themselves."
—Fort Collins Courier, July 7, 1921

* * * * * * *

- Harrison Avenue jeweler-1890
What happened to a Leadville jeweler on the night of February 13, 1881 is a mystery lost to the sands of time and the supernatural.
Denver Public Library Western History Collection, #10000379

* * * * * * *

PHANTOM PILFERS A SPARKLER

One February midnight in 1881, Dan Golding, a Leadville jeweler, was awakened in his house by the appearance of a lady in white who indicated that he should follow her out the door. Golding, surprised more than fear-struck, dressed quickly and hurried after the ghostly visitor. She led him down Harrison Avenue and stopped in front of Dan's jewelry store. Unlocking the door, he entered with the astral female and followed close behind her until she stopped by the door of the safe. When he opened the vault where the valuables were stored, the ghost at his side snatched an expensive ring, floated out of the store and down the street. Dan raced after the apparition, but was unable to catch the phantom thief. Heartbroken, he returned to the store, bolted the door and made his way back home. Dejectedly reporting to work the next morning, he went directly to the vault, opened it and found the stolen ring in its proper place.

* * * * * * *

"I have read a story of a woman whose ghost haunted her people because they made her grave clothes too short so that the fires of purgatory burned her knees."
--Creede Candle, March 11, 1922

* * * * * * *

STATE-STREET SPIRITUALISM

During Victorian times, Spiritualism was a popular religious practice in which mediums communicated with spirits of the dead. Its objective was to help human beings overcome the fear of death and view it not as the end of life but only a different phase of existence. It also promoted the belief that souls could attain higher levels of perfection in the world beyond the grave. Following the Civil War, spiritualist mediums perfected the art of making ghosts materialize out of a large wooden compartment known as a séance cabinet. While in a trance state, necromancers reportedly contacted the spirits of dead friends and family members who could give their living relations insights into the afterlife. Members of the audience who received messages or visits from the dead often left the sessions confident that the departed were not suffering eternal punishment, but instead were enjoying a world filled with more exquisite delights.

Leadville, like most other mining camps, was a favorite destination for a cabal of itinerant mediums, telepathists and hypnotists who plied their trade in the city well into the 20th Century.

* * * * * * *

"...for a short time they got down to the business of the evening, namely, electrifying spirits sufficiently to communicate with the mortals of this mundane sphere."
—*Leadville Daily Herald description of a séance held at an insurance office at Second and Harrison for the purpose of contacting a local judge who recently died.*

* * * * * * *

In 1882, a professional spiritualist by the name of Miller arrived in town to conjure up a few ghosts by gaslight. Hundreds attended the production, held at the Tabor Opera House. Among other things, the phantom minions carried flowers, wrote in blood and caused a piano and other musical instruments to float. They also walked among the crowd and greeted audience members who weren't afraid to grasp a cold, clammy hand.

Five years later, a Leadville reporter chronicled a typical metaphysical performance after a stranger approached him on the street late one night and asked if he believed in spiritualism. "Come with me," said the gentleman, who then led the scribe along the avenue, turned west to the foot of State Street and stopped in front of a log cabin. After tapping three times, the door swung wide and a petite, middle-aged woman admitted the pair, asking them to take a seat. The room was full of men and women, some of whom were believers in the supernatural. Others attended out of curiosity.

On one side of the chamber was a large walnut cabinet standing a couple of feet from the wall and in front of which chairs were arranged. A man named Mr. Burke, the "spirit guide", said conditions didn't favor visits from the spirit world because many people in the audience were uneasy. He introduced Mrs. Burke, the medium and the same woman who let spectators in the door. In response to generous applause, she bowed deeply and went to work, asking if anyone wanted to examine the séance cabinet. Several people inspected the box and found solid walls and back, no trapdoors or hidden pockets. A thin curtain hung in front of the entrance.

Mrs. Burke entered the cabinet and closed the curtain while her husband directed the audience to sing "Nearer, My God to Thee." Meanwhile, in the dim light of the cabin's interior the audience harmonized and waited in reverent expectation. Before the second verse was done, the curtains parted and the spirit of a beautiful woman appeared. It was "Priscilla", the ghost of a Greek maiden who came to bless those gathered within the room. She called a lady from the audience by name, and asking her to approach, spoke with her near the entrance of the cabinet.

Just then, the voice of "Little Bright Eyes", a spirit child who always attended the séances asked if there was a man present from Texas. A spectator near the back of the room answered in the affirmative, and Mr. Burke said there were spirits that wanted to speak with him. Burke described the ghosts and gave their names as each spoke to the man. The Texan recognized each one and its particular voice, but the most astonishing manifestations were the ghosts of Frank Cushman, a well-known but recently dead Leadville mining man and his sister. Frank called members of the audience to go forward and speak with him.

"Little Bright Eyes" made witty chatter the whole time while venturing several feet away from the front of the cabinet. When the news reporter approached her, she melted into thin air.

"There was not even a rag left," said the newsman. "This she repeated out on the floor in front of the cabinet several times. She faded away in a moment, not leaving a grease spot behind her. Whether a real spirit or the product of some trick, the phenomenon was surprising."

* * * * * * *

"No real generous man would go to a spiritual séance given by a lady medium, and just as the ghost is walking about (while the medium is tied in the cabinet) exclaim: 'There's a rat right by the ghost.' It spoils the effect to have the ghost yell and gather up its skirts and run."

—Boulder News and Courier, June 4, 1880

* * * * * * *

Onlookers were at a loss to explain how the spirits manifested or suddenly disappeared without a trace. At another point in the performance, two apparitions walked around the curtain. One was named Alicia Carey, who told a gentleman in the crowd that she was always nearby to guide and inspire him. Another was a tearful ghost, the ex-husband of a local variety show actress also in attendance. At times, several spirits materialized simultaneously, each speaking with a distinct voice, as did Mr. And Mrs. Burke, Priscilla, Little Bright Eyes and the other apparitions. Those present who received visits from departed friends and family members were convinced of the authenticity of the ghosts.

While believers in spiritualism were finding solace at séances throughout the city, the dark heart of Leadville's demimonde had a knack for laying the sweetest enticements as well as the most unspeakable horrors at the feet of unwary fortune seekers.

Urban Haunts

"What is the matter with our modern spirits, anyway? In a day when the world has gone mad on the subject of efficiency, why do we find our ghosts so utterly incompetent, so unequal to their jobs?"

—*Chaffee County Democrat, September 3, 1921*

* * * * * * *

WITCHES AND VAMPIRES IN THE MOUNTAINS

During Leadville's untamed youth, it was said that the vice of New York, Paris and London was not only reproduced but exaggerated in the cloud city's licentious precincts. Gas-lit streets led to somber alleyways of the city's nocturnal spheres—labyrinths replete with darting shadows, faceless voices and laughter, hollow moans, gunshots, oaths and other varieties of pandemonium that bubbled up from the depths of the West's most notorious underworld.

Quotations culled from the press of the 1880s suggest the existence of a sinister class of beings that frolicked in the darkness of the carbonate camp's purgatorial regions. Their victims were the careless, the inquisitive, the drunk or the drugged that dared to set foot into the alluring but forlorn passageways located behind the enterprises lining lower Harrison Avenue, State and Chestnut streets. News reports invite speculation as to the true nature of these entities.

"According to the officers the vampires of State Street, male and female, are bolder and more skillful in their work to-day than they have been for years past."

—*Leadville Daily and Evening Chronicle*

* * * * * * *

"The place was naturally an ideal paradise and one well calculated to soothe the tired spirit to a delicious rest, instead being converted into a scene of the most horrible crimes, of which, perhaps murder is one of the least. It had been selected by these human vampires not because of its almost supernatural beauty, but because of its isolated and lonely position the deeds of darkness planned almost daily, could be carried out with impunity and with but little fear of discovery."

—*Leadville Daily and Evening Chronicle*

* * * * * * *

"He had despaired of ever seeing them in the tentacles of the law, and then again he was somewhat exasperated at the infamous treachery of some Iscariot who had notified the vampires at the moment, the very moment the authorities were about to throw the cast net about them."

—*Leadville Daily Herald*

* * * * * * *

"Invoicing the situation the gentlemen descended on them just as they entered the dark mouth of the alley to perpetrate their nefarious designs, and saw the vampires vanish while their drunken victim was committed to Captain Roberts for protection."

—Leadville Daily and Evening Chronicle

* * * * * * *

"Marshal Jameson has been instructed to rid the city of these human vampires at once."

—Leadville Daily Herald

* * * * * * *

"Hall had exhausted his cash after a few sallies at the prizes, and searching into a pocket that was buried beneath the overhalls, produced a certificate of deposit endorsed by A.V. Hunter for $470. Upon the back the tenderfoot's signature was placed, while the vampires watched with flaming interest every curve of the pen."

—Leadville Daily and Evening Chronicle

* * * * * * *

"He was searched, and a pocketful of gold amounting to $210 was taken from him and deposited in the big iron vault, where it was at least temporarily secure from the vampires."

—Leadville Daily and Evening Chronicle

* * * * * * *

"I don't know what ever possessed the child—for she was provided with every comfort—unless it was the vampire that got hold of her."

—Leadville Daily and Evening Chronicle

* * * * * * *

"A better opportunity could not have been furnished the voracious vampires who were looking for a dainty diet, and as the dago tottered into the alley, they swept down upon him."

—Leadville Daily and Evening Chronicle

* * * * * * *

"It was not his fault that he awoke in the bowels of the bastile, but that of the vampires who had undertaken to teach him the arts and wiles of the sulphide city."

—Leadville Daily and Evening Chronicle

* * * * * * *

"He forgot when he was reveling before the witcheries of the Cyprian that there was a family depending on his resources; that in a fisherman's hut were infants who lived on a stinted allowance while he was casting his pearls before the vampires of the mountains."

—Leadville Daily and Evening Chronicle

* * * * * * *

"And what a formidable task it has been to protect himself from the vampires that dove-tailed themselves to him, and who conceived every variety of trickery and villainy for his downfall."

—*Leadville Daily and Evening Chronicle*

* * * * * * *

"The familiar story of the vampire and the verdant voyager was repeated at police headquarters at an early hour this morning."

—*Leadville Daily and Evening Chronicle*

* * * * * * *

"Positive facts…that the State Street vampire is invincible."

—*Leadville Daily and Evening Chronicle*

* * * * * * *

"To Maud Mealy, who is old in crime, a severe lesson should be administered, for as long as these vampires are tolerated on State Street so long will complaints of the present kind be registered."

—*Leadville Daily and Evening Chronicle*

* * * * * * *

"Had he been sober, his attention might have been attracted by the number of vampires whose eyes followed him."

—*Leadville Daily and Evening Chronicle*

* * * * * * *

A few years later, similar creatures also roamed the sporting district at Aspen, Leadville's silver-clad sister just across the western divide.

* * * * * * *

"All care to the winds we merrily fling,
The damp, cold grave is a dead-sure thing,
It's a dead-sure thing we're alive to-night,
And the damp, cold grave is out of sight."

—*Aspen Daily Leader*

* * * * * * *

"This is a bad state of affairs and robs of police of two-thirds of their power, giving at the same time a sort of protection to these vampires that prey upon the miner, the teamsters, the laborer, and, in fact, every class of men whose pluck and energy build up camps, wrest the riches from the mountains, and transform solitudes into scenes of busy life, and with whose push and enterprise these same vampires have not one whit of sympathy or kindly feeling."

—*Aspen Daily Chronicle*

"The officers are to be congratulated on their efforts to break up the gang of vampires who are living off the women of the half world, and it is the intention of the authorities to continue the work until the city is rid of the pest."

—Aspen Democrat

* * * * * * *

Witches also held sway over Leadvillians who believed in necromancy and other forms of the Black Arts, as quoted in a January 1910 edition of the Carbonate Chronicle, in which a pair of sorceresses battled over their pet bovines.

"Here in the shadow of the mountains the warp and woof of witchery is being wound around the very vitals of vigorous humans."

Sorcery was not uncommon in the Carbonate City, probably making its debut in Leadville with the arrival of eastern Europeans. Early Irish immigrants also knew a thing or two about the witchwife and her dreaded Circean wiles.

Tales of conjuration and wizardry occasionally surfaced in the newspapers of early Leadville, and an article entitled "Tied red ribbon on horns of cow—Terrible 'Bosorka' or Austrian Witchcraft Used by Zuzi, the Lorelei of the Danube", began with this tantalizing spell:

> "Double, double toil and trouble;
> Fire burn and cauldron bubble.
> Eye of newt and toe of frog,
> Wool of bat and tongue of dog.
> By the pricking of my thumbs,
> Something wicked this way comes."

Anna Bolna and Zuzi Bencko, both residents of lower Elm Street, where it dead-ended at City Cemetery, wound up in the court of Justice Connors to answer to charges of breaching the peace. During the hearing, as stated by a Slovenian interpreter, Anna said that Zuzi put a hex on her prized black milk cow, causing it to stop eating. Zuzi, also the owner of her own dusky milker, vigorously denied the accusation. She leveled a similar charge at her opponent and said that as a result of Anna's magic spell, her own animal kicked and the milk mysteriously turned black before it stopped flowing altogether. All this, she stated, took place after she found a strange red ribbon tied between Bossy's horns.

Friends and acquaintances representing both sides of the issue were at the hearing to lend support and if necessary, testify on behalf of the contestants. All were present except John Posivac, who the newspaper said was supposed to be a friend of Zuzi.

"He was to be her star witness and clear her of all connivance with weird and wandering witches."

Come time for the hearing, Posivac was nowhere to be found. He apparently became spooked after someone told him that Anna was a sorceress herself with no little witch power. Fearing that one or both of the women might summon some misfortune upon him after his testimony, he left town rather than run the risk bedevilment. For obvious reasons many neighborhood residents also avoided taking sides in the case.

"All the Austrian colony are discussing the affair," the news writer added, "But nobody is bellowing it from the housetops, for witches are at home in the upper air."

Caught as he was between a pair of cows and their female owners, each accusing the other of witchcraft, Connors rendered a most logical decision on such a highly esoteric matter.

"Inasmuch as there are two witches, two women and two black cows involved in this matter, it appears to me that John Posivac is the goat," the justice said. "I understand that John was to appear for Zuzi, but was apprised that he might suffer evil at the hands of Anna through the magic of the denizens of witchdom. Therefore, I decree that John will have to take care of himself and I will divide the costs of the action between you."

Sorcery wasn't the only hocus-pocus riding on the winds of Leadville's west side. Years earlier, a pair of vagabonds wandering through town, quickly learned that the city was indeed seething with spirits of the dead when they took shelter in an abandoned structure on West Chestnut.

* * * * * * *

Urban Haunts

"The clock strikes twelve; immediately Death begins to play an infernal waltz, the graves open and skeletons appear flitting hither and thither; the night is dark; the winter wind blows through the forest, yet the frightful skeletons clang their bones together in the weird dance. At the very height of their ghostly frolic the cock crows, summoning the dawn of day; immediately there is a rumbling of the earth, the graves open, the skeletons disappear, Death departs with a mournful declamation, and all is once more hushed in silence."

—*Colorado Springs Gazette*, October 13, 1877

✻ ✻ ✻ ✻ ✻ ✻

DARK DEEDS AT THE BRASS BONNET

Chestnut Street, shown here, had its unsavory side, but State, one block to the north, was the home of Shakespeare's "deed without a name".
Denver Public Library Western History Collection, X-11476

✻ ✻ ✻ ✻ ✻ ✻

By 1886, the trappings of civilization descended on Leadville but the tales of the good, not-so-old days were still fresh in the minds and on the tongues of pioneers. Sadly, the rough-and-tumble carbonate excitements of the early years were gone forever.

One stormy Friday evening during the summer of that year, a pair of tramps found refuge from approaching thunder and lightning in one of the deserted structures on lower Chestnut

Street where they could spend the night at no cost. Satisfied that they would not be disturbed, the wayfarers lit a candle and saw that the quarters they selected was a former saloon. They threw their worn bedrolls on the floor and slept for a time but were awakened by a crashing sound followed by groaning male and female voices, a gunshot and a scream eerie enough to make the blood run cold. The men bolted to their feet and saw nothing except a different shade of darkness through the broken windows and the occasional flash of lightning. Peering toward the far end of the lightless room, an unnatural yellowish incandescence appeared in a corner of the hall. It grew in intensity and soon the entire place was illuminated by an unearthly glow, revealing shadowy figures of men and women moving across the floor. More gunshots and hollow voices followed, occasionally punctuated by a scream.

"The sounds were interspersed with an unearthly and horrible kind of music to which the forms flitted around the frightened spectators in a veritable demon dance," said the news of the day in its description of the scene. "The horrible skeleton faces gliding hither and thither, leering at the two men with hideous grins as they passed them."

Petrified with fear and unable to move from their chosen spot not far from the dusty, dilapidated bar, the tramps cringed as the furious orgy swung in their direction and the whispy clothing of the dancers, the consistency of cobwebs, brushed at their unshaven faces. The pandemonium increased in intensity as they gazed in disbelief at the ghostly carnival.

"Soon, the din became more terrible," the press continued. "The movements of the waltzers quicker and quicker, and the sounds of screams, oaths and shots seemed to fill the whole apartment, gibbering skeletons gathered about them until in an agony of desperation the frightened men made a wild dash through the throng, and emerged from the entrance into the night with the cold sweat pouring from their faces and eyes almost staring from their sockets."

The pair didn't stop their sprint up Chestnut until they reached the light and human companionship of Harrison Avenue. The sounds of the demon dance and the thought of skeleton fingers grasping at their clothing seemed to follow them as they ran. Shocked after what they witnessed inside the derelict building, the pair sought refuge in an all-night café on Harrison. In their headlong rush from the unholy place, they forgot to pick up their beds.

Next morning, a group of men with the tramps in tow marched down Chestnut to investigate the spook-ridden building by the light of day. It was a long, narrow structure, a lifeless, decaying shell, said the Leadville Daily & Evening Chronicle, "…with the boards on the sides swinging with uneasy motion as the wind swept through the doorless entrances, moaning even then like the wailings of some lost spirits, occasionally fluttering from the sides fragments of some gaudy paper or decorations which had once gilded this palace of sin, bits of broken glass, flooring which, from the friction of many feet, had been in places worn through, like a skeleton of the past, was all that remained of what was once the greatest resort of the camp, where money had been poured out like water and wickedness ran riot throughout the hours of many a long night."

Devilment of the skeletal variety greeted an unsuspecting pair of vagrants who cast their bedrolls for the night in a former Chestnut Street den of iniquity. Dozens of ghostly establishments such as these in the old Leadville business precinct could offer up provocative autobiographies.
Image courtesy of History Colorado Photograph Collection, #10038242

Following inquiries among some of the early pioneers to Leadville, it was learned that the "Brass Bonnet", as the palace was called in bygone days, was one of the most renowned dance halls in the West, famous for the crowds of customers who patronized it and for the numbers of shootings and calamities that occurred there. Some of the dark deeds and crimes that took place were of a kind never imagined, even in the vice-ridden city of Leadville. A number of men known to carry large amounts of money went through its doors but reportedly never emerged. It was believed they were murdered, robbed, and their bodies buried on the property or left in a nearby corral to be devoured by pigs.

Neighbors corroborated the story told by the vagrants, saying that beginning at midnight and continuing until the early hours of morning, they frequently saw the ghostly light emanating from the decaying dance hall and heard strains of unearthly music carried on the wind. No one dared approach the building, and travelers along Chestnut gave the place a wide berth, taking another route to their destination or walking on the opposite side of the street until well past the accursed spot.

"Passing through the Chestnut Street of today one marvels at the change. Stores, banks, commission houses, hotels, saloons, dance halls and theaters, where the sound of revelry and music was ever present night and day, where the large gains of the day were spent like water at night, and the sounds of the dealer's voice mingled with gay laughter and boisterous enjoyment, all now deserted and as still and quiet as the grave, the buildings empty and dismantled, fitting homes for the ghosts of the past, with which the mind cannot help peopling them."
—Leadville Daily & Evening Chronicle, July 22, 1886

* * * * * * *

MINER BILL COMES TO CALL

Bill Jackson put off mortality in 1883 the day falling rock and timbers truncated portions of his anatomy as he shoveled muck at the bottom of the Nisi Prius Shaft atop Rock Hill. He went peacefully to his six-foot bungalow at Evergreen following the usual post-mortem obsequies but returned from the dead a year later when a group of Leadville table-tippers parted the celestial veil and summoned his shade back to the New York Club.

Very early one Tuesday morning after the whirring roulette wheels fell silent and the clicking chips and rattling dice were retired from the green felt tables, club proprietor John Pentand and his friends assembled for their nightly séance. Dousing their cigars and dimming the lights, the half-dozen faithful spiritualists took seats around a table and commenced a ritual designed to call up spirits from the abode of the dead.

"Stygian darkness prevailed," said a Leadville newspaper. "Soon mysterious sounds were heard, hands were passed lightly over their heads and brushed their cheeks. Weird music was heard in the distance, growing fainter and fainter and then louder till it seemed hovering over their heads."

As quickly as it began, the phantom aria stopped and in the tomb-like silence, shadowy forms of restless souls from the netherworld materialized and flitted around the room. After several minutes, these also evaporated and the roulette wheel with its tiny ivory ball began spinning at the command of unseen hands. When luck drew the ball into its appointed slot, the wheel coasted to a stop and stillness once again descended on the room where the spectators sat in nervous expectation.

"They almost forgot to breathe," the news report added. "And the ticking of their watches sounded like blows upon an anvil, the silence was so great."

When a pale yellow light began to emanate through the doorway of an adjoining room, two members of the group got up to investigate. It quickly faded and the terrified men made rapid strides back to the company of their friends. Surveying the ghostly spectacle, the men watched the eerie glow and gliding figures reappear, but this time they were joined by the pallid figure of Mr. Jackson, the late-lamented miner who was mangled the previous year in California Gulch. Several of the occultists who knew Bill in life identified his ghost as it stood reassembled and motionless among the other discarnate entities drifting over the floorboards.

One of the watchers, nerves shattered by the unearthly scene, called for Mr. Pentand to raise the lights. As the gas lamps were ignited, the weirdness dissolved and the mystical conclave ended. Regaining their composure with a parting drink and cigars, the spirit rappers, all Leadville attorneys, agreed to let the uncanny proceedings rest until another night.

* * * * * * *

"Spiritual séances are still raging among the believers of visits from the disembodied spirits of the dead. The ghostly visitors range all the way from Judas Iscariot down to Frodsham, and indulge in all sorts of antics. They are not as a rule a very sedate set of ghosts; but are even more lively than they were in the flesh. These séances are not for gain, but simply 'for intelligent development' and a good time."

—Leadville Daily Herald, October 3, 1884

* * * * * * *

NYMPHS FROM THE NETHERWORLD

Molly May was the Cloud City's most resplendent mistress. Her life before Leadville was a telling preamble to what awaited her in the Rocky Mountains. Swearing off an upstanding Midwestern lifestyle, she drifted West in the early 1870s, finally landing in Cheyenne at McDaniels' Vaudeville Theater. It was there that she began to entertain the thirsty cowboys and freighters who wandered in from the plains.

"She began her wayward career, and leaving the golden paths of an old home in Illinois, she was soon in the maelstrom of the frontier," said an early Leadville newspaper of Mollie's westward pilgrimage.

Seduced by new gold discoveries, the prospect of capturing some of the profits lured her north to the Black Hills in 1876.

"Here she seized the scepter from her rivals and reigned as queen," the biographer continued. "Scores worshiped at her shrine."

It wasn't long until Miss May fell in over her head with Jim May, the elder of a pair of brothers. Not to be outdone, his younger sibling "Boone" May, the famed shotgun messenger of the Cheyenne & Black Hills Stage and Express Company, succumbed to the curse of Cain. Coveting the alluring Mollie, he fired a shot at his brother as the couple socialized in the bar of the Gem Theater. Usually a dead shot, May's projectile went a little wide and hit Mollie in the midsection, but miraculously its fatal flight was diverted by a steel flange in her corset.

Shortly after her brush with the leaden messenger of death, an otherwise amiable carriage ride with a female acquaintance turned sour and Mollie lost part of her left ear to the teeth of Fanny Garretson in a dispute that apparently began over the affections of a Deadwood banjo player known as James Brown. When an Irish comedian named Shaughnessy also claimed Mollie for his own, Brown promptly settled the matter when he shot and killed the comic center-stage at the Melodian Concert Hall.

Brown's bid for the lovely Miss May failed and Mollie decided it was time to foreswear the violence of Deadwood and strike out for the Rocky Mountains to sample what Leadville had to offer. Once in the city above the clouds, Miss May lost no time putting down permanent roots, and ordered construction to begin immediately on her own place of business.

Rising from the sagebrush-covered flat between West Fourth and Fifth streets in 1879, Molly May's gilded palace of sin was said to be the first two-story building on Harrison Avenue. When the stained glass, brass trimmings and lacy millwork were added, it became one of the most imposing and opulent structures in the vigorous mining town of Leadville. In September of that year, it was among the first 100 businesses to get telephone service, along with Sheriff Tucker's office, Rogers' Undertaking Rooms and the Leadville Water Company.

Miss May quickly filled her casino to the upper floors with the finest school of nymphs the territory had to offer, most of whom carried the tidy titles of Belle, Minnie, Birdie, Fannie, Frankie and Hattie.

When more respectable establishments also began springing up along Harrison, the May emporium was banished from the main thoroughfare and moved to 129 Park Avenue (now West Fifth), where it shared the block with other bagnios operated by Winnie Purdy, Sally Purple and Mollie Price.

Park Avenue, especially Mollie's place, had a checkered history and was the scene of many a scarlet saturnalia and assorted homicides during Leadville's first decade of existence. Despite the occasional bump on the road to riches, the fashionable red-light district flourished.

"It is not many years since nearly every house in the block was given over to the followers of the scarlet woman," penned a Leadville reporter in 1886 after a visual assessment of the Park Avenue playground.

Mollie May, like most of her rivals, loved diamonds and was seldom seen when she wasn't heavily bedecked with beautiful sparklers. She rarely drank in excess except for one February evening in 1883, when she imbibed more than her usual quota and became very drunk. Police were called to a free-for-all between Mollie, her partner and an army of girls. Miss May was promptly arrested and escorted to jail, but en-route, she collapsed in the snow and refused to budge. Being a rather large, heavy woman, it took three burly cops and a couple of helpful civilians, one at each limb and another at her head, to carry Madame May to the city lockup.

"She shrieked and cursed along the street until the air rang with the sound of her voice, and crowds ran out to see what was the matter," said the local newspaper report following the incident. "The police got some pretty hard raps in the struggle." Following the street-side wrestling match, the officers agreed that Mollie was a force to reckon with, one that could kick harder than a Missouri mule and scratch more like a wildcat than a human. After a night in jail, Judge Rose fined Mollie $75 and sent her home.

On the evening of January 30, 1883, things took an incindiary twist when a blaze that started in a neighboring bordello threatened Mollie May's place. The fire laddies arrived, and the girls, many of whom were dressed only in the airy draperies of Venus, were running around the street in a wild manner. The flames consumed the two neighboring bagnios to the west before it was extinguished. Miss May's casino received only water damage.

Wars between rival madams were common and no doubt Mollie was thrilled that two of her competitors were temporarily out of business. Following particularly heated battles, they frequently dragged one another into court demanding justice, with the plaintiff inevitably accusing the defendant of keeping a house of ill-fame.

Mollie's place had a stormy history from the start, and many who were associated with the establishment died or were murdered sooner rather than later. Numbered among them were James Burns the faro dealer, Jim Kinney, the paramour of Belle Jewell, who took over the business after Mollie's death, Morgan Courtney, a prominent but rather unsavory mine manager from Australia, and "Buck" Lee, another landlord.

Shortly after Kinney crossed the Dark River, spiritual visitants appeared at the May manor. Many residents reported ghostly footfalls throughout the house and dim outlines of the astral visitors in the many mirrors that adorned its walls. In the years following Mollie's demise, Belle claimed that on more than one occasion she was horrified to see the ghosts of Mollie and Mr. Kinney reflected in their glass during the early morning hours. Numerous inmates of Mollie's palace also met an untimely end, many within the walls of the house. When Miss Jewell left the business, Laura LeClair managed the enterprise for a time, but died while on a trip to Denver. Ollie Patterson purchased the property for $4,000 and ran the bordello before turning it over to Jessie Lester, who for a time brought back the glitter of the early years. When Ollie returned, Jessie went to Creede where she died of pneumonia one night during a drinking and gambling debauch. Miss Patterson wasn't long for this world either. She died a horrible death after drinking carbolic acid while involved in a stormy love affair. Over the next few years, no fewer than nine other muses, including 18-year old Rosa Howard, set sail for the Stygian shore while engaged at the May mansion.

As a result, many employees and patrons asserted that the palace of joy was haunted, home to many of the lost souls who put off mortality there. It was on Miss Jewell's watch that ghosts began to stalk the May house in sufficient numbers and frequency to completely unnerve residents.

One new arrival from San Francisco was fast asleep when she felt an icy hand caress her face. She awoke to see a ghostly female leaning over her bed. Not at all amused at the prospect of sharing her room with anyone in immortal form, the terrified woman left Leadville the next day in the company of several of her wayward sisters.

Mollie May died April 10, 1887 of a heart ailment. The mourners, mainly members of the Park Avenue sorority, displayed their grief with mournful weeping and a mountain of flowers that completely obscured the casket. A new $3,000 hearse purchased from a company in New Orleans carried the coffin and its tenant to last rites at the burial site.

"They all accompanied the remains to their last resting place," said an 1887 edition of the Leadville Daily and Evening Chronicle. "Nor could their final tributes to their departed sister have been more solemn or impressive. And yet they were waifs, outcasts, whom the general public has been taught that in their lives the last vein of tenderness has run dry, the last flower of childhood chilled and frosted. It's a strange lesson."

The bereaved left Mollie's corpse at Evergreen that spring afternoon but her shade lingered in the rooms and hallways of Number 129. It seems that the mysterious disappearance of her prized diamond collection served to hasten Mollie's ghostly return to Leadville. When asked, no one seemed to know what became of the jewels, but most surmised that they were stolen. Even before the mound of cut flowers left on Miss May's grave began to wilt away, the ghost of the dead madam began its nocturnal meanderings in search of the missing treasure.

One evening while sitting in her room, Belle heard a knock at the door. Opening it, she found no one there, but instead felt an icy blast of air blow past her and into the chamber. She closed the door, and perceiving she was not alone, felt presences wandering about, as if searching the room. Miss Jewell said it was the spirit of Mollie May looking for her lost gems. Others claimed that she returned from the dead because of an unfulfilled promise.

On her death bed, the head mistress made the girls pledge they would tend her grave, but they failed to live up to the agreement and her burial place was neglected. Mollie's restless soul, the girls lamented, was doomed to walk the corridors of her residence until the grave was maintained.

After the final solemnities and a failed attempt to maintain the plot, Mollie May's resting place remains unmarked and untended beneath a carpet of decaying pine needles. On West Fifth, the Leadville Post Office, the Elk's Club and a few humble residences populate the block where gilded carnivals once reigned supreme and where Miss May's ghost still drifts, disconsolate at the sad state of affairs.

Urban Haunts

Leadville's Evergreen Cemetery, where many an earthbound spirit is said to linger, offers solitude, a glimpse of Colorado history and the occasional encounter of the paranormal variety.
Photo by Mark Fox

WHEN THE CLOCK STRUCK THREE

"For some years, Leadville has been lacking in that most sensational of all sensational things—a haunted house," said an 1888 Leadville daily. "In the early days of the camp this want was supplied in the numerous specter-visited mines, cabins, etc., about the hills, but until recently the city itself has never actually known a spook-invested building."

Through mid-October of that year, much talk centered on a West Fifth Street house of joy that was the site of spectral visitations for three years running. Owners of the residence managed to keep the haunting a secret until the story eventually appeared in the newspaper.

In 1883, a well-known daughter of Leadville's tenderloin district expressed an interest in buying the house. The owner agreed to sell, but because the purchaser couldn't pay cash, she signed an agreement to make monthly payments.

After the last installment, or what the buyer believed to be the last was made, the woman left for Denver and there contracted smallpox. The disease produced fatal results and she was buried in the capitol city. After her death, the seller stated that the final payment on the house was never made, and despite claims of the dead woman's relatives, the property ended up in the hands of the original owners.

After the buyer's death, eerie manifestations authored by the dead woman's ghost, not at all pleased with the outcome of the purchase, began to take place in the room in which she used to live. Anyone who spent the night in her quarters refused to sleep there again and others, who couldn't bear the thought of sharing the same house with spirits, moved out completely.

Early in October, a new arrival to Leadville moved into the room with one of the other girls. After their first saturnalian evening on the town, they retired at 1 a.m. but were awakened by the sound of the clock striking three.

"Although it was in the middle of summer, and the apartment seemed perfectly warm when we went to bed—I having opened a window to let the pure air enter—a terrible chill seemed to pervade the room, and I experienced an almost icy coldness," one of the boarders told the newspaper reporter.

Getting up to lower the window, the new resident was surprised when it flew back up after a few moments. She pulled down the window once more, but again the frame flew open. This was repeated several more times, but always it was flung upward. Thinking the pulley was broken and not realizing that it was only the ghost protesting the fraudulent real estate transaction, she gave up and pulled down the curtain, but it too rolled up immediately with a noise that woke her roommate. Together the women pulled the curtain down and pushed a trunk against it to hold it in place. As they walked across the floor toward their beds, the curtain once again rolled up, slapping the wood repeatedly as it spun to a stop at the top of the frame. Returning to the window, they saw that the trunk was moved three inches away from the wall. Eight more times the pair was foiled at attempts to wedge the curtain between the wall and trunk.

On the ninth attempt ice-cold air filled the room and drove the lodgers back to the warmth of their beds. When they were about to go downstairs and procure more blankets or get another room, the chamber began to glow with a faint yellowish light. It revealed the dim outlines of the sparse furniture before fading to red, a greenish hue, then to a yellow-red color. Watching from their pillows, the ladies were horrified to see the pallid face of a female appear at the foot of their beds. They recognized the apparition, surrounded by hair, as that of the woman who purchased the house and who died in Denver. One of the girls screamed and raced for the door, followed by her companion. Opening it with difficulty, the nightgown-clad pair dashed through the hallway and down the stairs to the landlady's room, where they told the matron what happened.

"What! Have you seen it too?" the woman asked, handing them a key to another room. Despite the change of quarters, they didn't sleep the rest of the night.

Over the next few months, several other girls occupied the haunted room, each complaining of the same eerie phenomena. One woman said the window rattled all night and that the bed moved under its own power from its place against the wall to the center of the floor. While she saw no face, all occupants of the room experienced the ordeal of the window and curtain, and most witnessed the apparition of the moribund visage leering at them from the foot of the bed.

* * * * * * *

"Haunted houses can be curtainless and still have shades."

—*Creede Candle, August 10, 1918*

* * * * * * *

NO BELIEVER IN HOODOOS

"No, I don't believe in spiritualism, but I've been of late seeing and hearing strange things and I firmly believe them to be heavenly manifestations", said a late 19th-Century Leadvillite named Aunty Stewart to an Evening Chronicle reporter in December 1889 when ghosts were visiting the Carbonate City with eerie regularity.

On Thanksgiving Day she was sitting by the stove thinking about her departed son and wishing he could join her for the holiday meal. At that moment, she told the reporter, he appeared to her dressed in a long, flowing white robe and wearing a pair of white wings that dragged on the floor. Looking at his mother, he smiled, glided through the bedroom and disappeared into a wall. On another occasion he came and spoke to her, saying he was in the fourth heaven, where he would stay for a time before moving higher. The young phantasm described it as a beautiful place with flowers, trees and rivers, where everyone lived together in peace. The purpose of his return, he said, was to protect her, and he told her that before long she would join him in heaven.

"I'm no believer in hoodoos, but I saw Isaac just as plain as I see you," she told the reporter.

The newspaper speculated on the story and Isaac's celestial home somewhere between Leadville and the realm of the dead.

"Believers in spiritualism may be able to converse with Ike. As from all accounts he seems perfectly willing to leave that beautiful home and talk with the people of the Cloud City."

Urban Haunts

Standing trackside near this spot stood the haunted cottage in which the ghost of a tormented mother and the spirit of a railroad suicide wailed nightly. The house is gone, but the sound of forlorn sobs, sighs and bitter weeping can still take the late-night pedestrian by surprise.
Author's collection

* * * * * * *

Urban Haunts

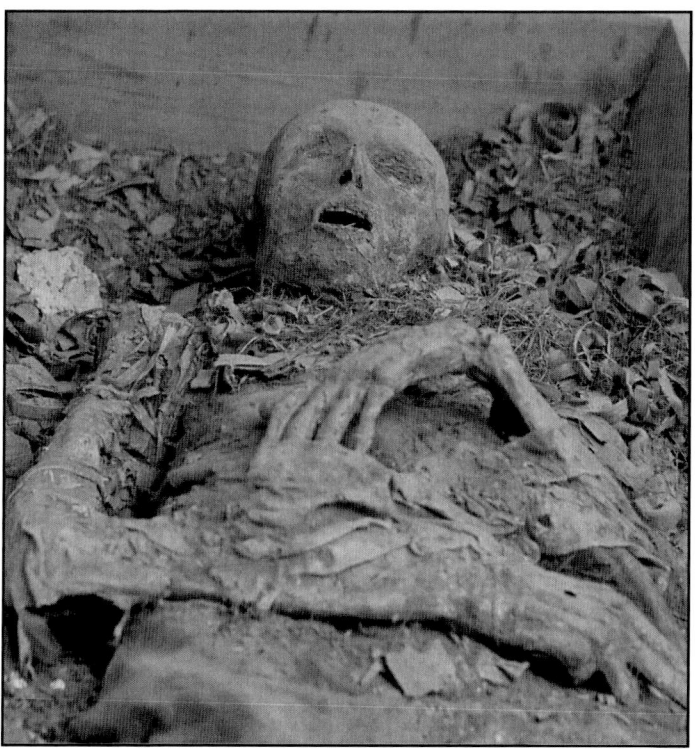

"When people are murdered, and their bodies (as often happens) are buried in cellars or other damp places, their ghosts, for the chemical reasons already given, are particularly likely to walk."

—*Oak Creek Times, November 3, 1910*

BONES IN THE CELLAR

As the 20th Century dawned in Colorado, another curious haunting rattled around Leadville in December 1900. Whether the case would ultimately prove to implicate a dead mother in a crime, strengthen a belief in spiritualism in the Cloud City or simply furnish another job for the coroner was never brought to light. However, the curious facts surrounding the disturbing tale and the identification of another haunted house in Leadville made it a curious ghost story.

"The house from which the mystery may come is No. 328 East Tenth Street," said a turn-of-the-century reporter from the Carbonate Chronicle. "It is a modest yet ornate little cottage, which stands alongside the South Park railroad track near the junction of what would be a continuation of Hazel and Tenth Street."

Occupying the home during that year was George Schafer, a self-proclaimed spiritualist and aspiring president of the Leadville Occult Society, at whose meetings visitors from beyond death's door were frequent guests, said a Leadville newspaper of the society's regular gatherings.

"There the disembodied spirits appear in great numbers and are viewed by an astonishingly large number of Leadville citizens, some of whom converse with them in the silent language of the spirit land, and describe them to their earthly friends with absolute accuracy."

Mrs. Schafer shared her husband's beliefs and said she personally witnessed many paranormal manifestations that helped convince her of the existence of apparitions from beyond the grave.

"Once is Kansas City," she said, "While walking up Main Street of that city, I was struck by some obscure object and knocked down. The stun was only momentary and I have never to this day been able to account for the strange occurrence. I am of the belief, however, that it was something in spirit form passing through the air which came in contact with me."

Erected in 1881 by a carpenter named Christensen, Number 328's builder occupied the home for the next decade until it became a rental property. Schafer and his family moved into the residence during the summer of 1900, but the family that previously occupied it said a haunting was the reason they left. Even though Mr. Schafer was an enthusiastic believer in anything of an otherworldly nature, he said that ghosts were not the reason he was moving into the haunted cottage. As far as he was concerned, resident spirits or hobgoblins only served to enhance the value of the property. The lease was signed without delay and the little family took occupancy hoping that the uncanny inhabitants would make their appearance just as quickly.

As soon as the couple finished unpacking their belongings, strange knockings emanated from the walls and floating spirits drifted around the rooms in the middle of the night.

Apparently, the cellar of the house was the abode in which the ghostly presences were held captive, and there that physical evidence could be found that could verify their existence.

It was claimed that in 1887 a pregnant woman lived in the house, and several weeks after the child was born, she murdered it. According to reports, no funeral was held. Instead, the mother buried the baby's body in the basement, where the bones remained at the time Schafer and his wife took occupancy. The Carbonate Chronicle suggested that the shade of the child's mother might be responsible for the spiritual unrest occurring nightly at the house.

"Spiritual mediums who are interested in the case as well as the residents of the house claim that a ghost in the form of the mother of the child, who died some years ago and is buried in Evergreen Cemetery, haunts the house by night and raves in her remorse for her crime and is restless because the child does not repose at her side in the cemetery instead of the cold damp cellar of the East Tenth Street cottage."

Three years after the tragedy, another phantom, the shade of a man who committed suicide on the Rio Grande tracks 20 ft. west of the house, also took up residence in the home.

So intriguing were the circumstances of the haunting, that members of the Leadville Occult Society took a personal interest in the investigation of the case. A member of the group, an acclaimed hypnotic healer and master of universal thought by the name of Professor Blinn agreed to help uncover the truth behind the spectral visitations.

Blinn's favorite hypnotic subject, a woman named Mrs. Ivory, agreed to help with the experiment by allowing herself to be placed into a trance. While in mesmerized slumber, she communicated with the deceased mother of the dead child. The mother told Ivory that her child's bones were beneath the cellar floor and asked that members of the Occult Society go there, dig up the body and inter it in Evergreen. A member of the Leadville press was invited to assist in the sojourn to the cellar to locate the baby's remains.

The following afternoon, the excavators, armed with pick and shovel, descended into the basement to search for their quest. After 30 minutes work, the tools had barely made a dent in the hard, compacted floor of the cellar. The diggers agreed to put off further work until the exact location of the bones was provided and more efficient implements could be procured.

Today, Number 328, the trackside tenement that contained the makeshift grave and resident specters is gone. Whether digging resumed at a later date or if the bones were ever discovered remains a mystery only known to the ghosts of mother, child and the astral ranks of the Leadville Occult Society.

* * * * * * *

"The only ghosts who creep into this world are dead young mothers, returned to see how their children fare. There is no other inducement great enough to bring the departed back."

—The Durango Democrat, March 28, 1903

* * * * * * *

'REPENT OR DIE'

Two weeks after the disdainful ghost of a homicide victim stalked the alley behind the Saddle Rock Restaurant, and three weeks following the appearance of a forlorn and bleeding spirit at the Midland Depot, a Leadville police officer reported an ominous early-morning apparition in his home in the 100-block of West Seventh Street.

Deputy Tom Riley, generally considered to be a clear-thinking, conservative lawman, retired early one August night in 1892 and soon was dead to the world in the arms of Morpheus. At 2:30 a.m., roused by a strong gust of cold air caressing his face, Riley awoke thinking he was dreaming, since all the doors and windows in the house were closed. When the covers under which he slept slowly began migrating toward the foot of the bed, Riley realized that forces other than his mind were at work. Grabbing the blankets, he returned them to their place under his chin, but relaxing his grasp on the bedclothes, they once again started creeping down the bed.

After the errant sheets began their third trip towards the footboard Riley grew weary of the unusual game. Sitting up and looking toward the bedroom door, he saw a gentleman with long gray hair, beard and glowing eyes staring at him.

Asking the stranger what he wanted, the deputy listened as the phantom made a baleful gesture and informed him to mend his ways or he would soon find the Angel of Death knocking at his door.

With that dire prophecy, the phantom stood staring for some time and saying nothing before finally dissolving into the darkness. Tom didn't sleep the rest of the night, tossing, turning and thinking about the sinister forecast from the strange being. Details of the evil ways Riley was advised to swear off were never revealed, but the late-night visitation made the doubting deputy a steadfast believer in ghosts.

* * * * * * *

> "The spooks and goblins that delight
> To fill with terror all the night;
> That stalks abroad in hideous dreams
> With which dyspepsia's fancy teems,
> Will never trouble with their ills
> The man who trusts in Pierce's Pills.
> Dr. Pierce's Pleasant Purgative Pellets—vegetable, harmless, painless, sure!"

--Leadville Daily & Evening Chronicle, August 20, 1888

* * * * * *

PHANTOM MANIPULATION

Old Man Chernock lived in a "beautiful summer cottage out along the gulch somewhere", said a Leadville newsman in his description of the man's spartan, pine slab-encrusted shanty that clung precariously to the banks of California Bar.

A former county employee, Chernock was an aging recluse who developed a hearing problem and was eventually laid off of his job when he became a liability for the local government. As a result, the county was paying to feed Chernock, who came down from the gulch once every seven days to attend board meetings, thank the commissioners for their generosity and register his weekly complaint.

Making his way back to the dismal cabin in the gulch following meetings, the wind in the pines and the gurgling of the miserable little stream that trickled by the homestead usually lulled the old prospector into peaceful sleep.

The weekly ritual continued for many months until one Saturday night when he awoke to the sound of rapping at the cabin door. Passing off the noise as the tapping of a low-hanging branch, the nocturnal gnawing of some peckish rodent or the doings of some late-night pedestrian along the gulch road, Chernock mumbled a malediction, rolled over and dozed off. The knocking continued until well after midnight, when the vaporous shade of his late-departed former mining partner finally oozed through the door, pulled up a chair at the foot of the bed and struck up a conversation that lasted until 3 a.m.

For weeks the visitations continued and Mr. Chernock took his ghostly grievance to the sympathetic ears of the Leadville police, saying the long-winded spook was depriving him of valuable sleep. Officers listened patiently and even visited the residence occasionally, but the nightly nuisance persisted. The weary man decided to push the case before the county commissioners in hopes that its members could offer some relief from his unworldly insomnia.

At the mid-July 1898 board meeting, there was little business to conduct, so the gathering adjourned early to hear what Mr.

Chernock had to say. Expecting to be regaled with the man's customary rant, the commissioners were curiously surprised when his speech took a supernatural twist. The county fathers listened intently as he described the ghost who brought news from the netherworld about mining claims and revealed to him the location of rich strikes to be found in the area. Chernock proposed that if the commissioners would grubstake him, he could make enough money for the county to pay its $1.5 million debt.

Skeptically, the board members said they couldn't help and referred Chernock to one Dr. Couce, a visiting occultist from Washington who reportedly knew more about spooks than anybody and who could possibly lay the long-winded late-night spook to rest.

* * * * * * *

"Mrs. Clark, who resides in the alleged haunted house at 236 West Fifth Street has received more calls in the last few days than for many months before. No more than a few dozens of them dared enter the house. A few more of them dared go nearer than the width of the street where they would stand with open eyes and mouth ajar, showing by their side glances that they had selected a nice level place over which to run should anything get after them."
—The Herald Democrat, October 18, 1900

* * * * * * *

Urban Haunts

Drifting up and down Leadville's eastside streets in their mysterious nightwalks, unearthly women in black kept neighborhood residents shivering behind locked doors in the closing years of the 19th Century. Long-dead residents of these homes on East Sixth Street surely believed that the dreaded apparitions stalking the lanes were the harbingers of doom.

OCTOBER 1889

During the 1880s witch scare, when stories of black magic whistled around the eaves of Leadville homes, superstitious residents of the upper-east side were leery of anyone wandering the streets late at night. Hobgoblins lurked in shadows between houses, the banshee wailed on windy nights and conjurers cooked potions in black cauldrons in every block. Late-night pedestrians made fast tracks homeward, believing the woman in black followed close on their heels.

In the weeks leading up to Halloween 1889, a mysterious woman prowling neighborhood streets terrified East Leadville townsfolk.

"The woman dresses in black, with a long black veil which covers her face and reaches down to her knees," the news report said. "She appears on the streets about 11 o'clock at night and remains for several hours, sneaking back and forward."

Occasionally seen sitting on porches of neighborhood homes, she succeeded in scaring the life out of everyone who encountered her. One courageous soul approached the woman to ask what she wanted, to which the foreboding reply was "I want you!"

Aghast at the response, the questioner ran into the nearest house and the unearthly female passed up the darkened lane.

One Saturday night, a committee of curious neighborhood gentlemen laid in wait for the apparition but she failed to appear. There was no end to the speculation concerning her activity. Given her tall stature, some believed her to be a man dressed in woman's clothing, seeking to revenge a wrong. A diminutive footprint found in the mud debunked the theory, and others suggested she might be the dreaded banshee of Irish legend, come to presage a death in the neighborhood. A few even surmised that she could be an agent of London's butcher of Whitehall, whom many believed was planning to carve a bloody swath through Leadville's red-light district

"She flits along the sidewalk with a noiseless tread, and this adds to the mystery," the newspaper continued. "Some, of course, have advanced the theory that she is an emissary of the celebrated 'Jack', but, if so, she would have no occasion to be in the neighborhood she has visited, as the people who live up there are all good, honest folks."

Never seen except around the midnight hour, most believed the mysterious woman to be a spirit from beyond the grave. Only a few brave neighborhood boys dared to follow her from a safe distance, always losing sight of her among the houses and mine dumps of the east side. With her face always hidden behind the veil, the shadowy pedestrian avoided people during her nocturnal ramblings.

Hearing the news of the late-night phantom walker, Leadville police looked into the matter. Officer Telfer, hiding himself in the shadow of a building next to Starr Ditch waited along the specter's path. Just as she passed, the officer stepped out of the shadows and asked what her business was.

"I am not hurting anyone," she said.

Telfer went on to inform the apparition that her nightly meanderings were scaring neighborhood residents out of their wits. He asked her name.

"I have not intended to scare them," she replied, refusing to give her name or lift the veil from her face. She said her nightly excursions were an effort to walk off the sorrow at the recent death of her father. To the neighbors' relief, she agreed to return home and stop the nightly wanderings.

Further investigation revealed that the secretive hiker lived on East Eighth Street.

"The woman is probably slightly demented, but not to any great degree," said a newspaper reporter. "She is young and not all all ill-looking and the death of her father is probably the cause of her strange actions. It is certain she intended no harm."

Memories of the mysterious dark damsel persisted well into the 20th-Century, when years of oral tradition transformed her into the widow of a man killed in the Penrose Mine, located on the brow of Chicken Hill between East Third and Fourth streets. Legends told how the woman, dressed entirely in black, would wait at the mine for a husband that would never come up from the depths.

"Neighborhood children once placed a black flag on the mine dump," said longtime Leadville resident Howard Tritz. "One day it got twisted around the pole and everybody thought the Lady in Black was up there. Even the old widows in the neighborhood were outside looking at it."

* * * * * * *

"I had a hair brush and tried to brush the blue cat ghost off the footboard of my bed, but ghost cat would not vanish; the brush passed through it as it would have passed through a moonbeam. I blew at the ghost and it flickered as a flame flickers in a draft, but it remained where it had been. If anything it glowed a brighter blue. My own hair and my mustache were standing erect, and the hairs of my mustache tickled my nose and made me sneeze repeatedly. I sneezed right through the cat ghost each time, and this bent him into odd curves."

—*Longmont Ledger*, May 3, 1907

* * * * * * *

'OCCASIONAL STRANGE THINGS'

For the second time in its long history, something strange began flitting around the Lake County Courthouse during the spring of 2004. For one week, reports of the oddest sort emanated from the local lockup, where sheriff's employees and a pair of prisoners told of bizarre happenings that left even the most skeptical cops scratching their heads.

"There have been occasional strange things that have transpired here in the past," said Sheriff Ed Holte who presided over the unusual episodes. "This is an old jail, and considering the things that have gone on in here, I accept that it's possible, but I haven't seen it."

Jail inmates, largely skeptical about things supernatural, were quickly convinced that spirits of the dead returned to haunt the lockup. Increasing in intensity and frequency throughout the week, the otherworldly activity culminated with the recording of disembodied voices on tape and a closet full of freak physical manifestations that pointed to the presence of an unseen visitor from the nether realm.

Occupying cells on the west side of the jail and isolated from the general inmate population, the trusties busied themselves with a variety of daily tasks around the jail and courthouse, including cooking, cleaning and other odd jobs. Beginning the last week in May, a television used by the pair began acting up, the screen changing to blue and switching on and off rapidly. The glitch was passed off as a malfunction of the appliance. Later, when an extension cord and television cord unplugged themselves without human intervention and the television set swiveled to face another direction, the men began to wonder if a pesky poltergeist might be at work in their cells.

After dinner the same evening, one of the trusties returned to his room and was greeted by a drastic drop in temperature in the hallway just outside the cell. He noticed that objects in the room were moved from one place to another, apparently by supernatural means.

In the following days, the entity not only continued to focus its attention on the television, but also forcefully unplugged cords in plain sight, moved and stacked objects, left a cryptic message in small adhesive letters and created a hand-knotted cross of nylon cord. The trusty showed the creation to jail employees and hung it over the door to the cell. He left briefly but returned to find the cross missing. A search of the entire jail for the object turned up nothing.

Evidence of the invisible intruder also appeared on tape recordings, and featured the chilling sounds of a disembodied male voice uttering whispers, moans, whistles and choking sounds, as well as the phrases "Bless me!" and "Higher!"

Ghostly mischief continued for one week, then stopped as quickly as it began. Inmates suggested the possibility that former prisoners who died after the jail's construction in the 1950s could be responsible for the activity.

Stranger still is how events in history can repeat themselves, even across a span of more than a century.

Phantoms inhabiting the Lake County Jail environs are nothing new, and the 2004 activity is one of the most recent in a long line of unearthly events at the Leadville courthouse. In the late 19th Century, similar events plagued the inhabitants of the original lockup, terrifying them into hysterics after they were placed in haunted cells. Even though the original Victorian-era courthouse was demolished following a fire in 1942, the disembodied spirits of jail suicides still haunting the area might be responsible for the present-day spookiness.

* * * * * * *

"A rumor was circulated in and around the county jail that the ghost of 'Old Hank,'… was flitting around his old quarters, having died in the jail but a short time prior to the eighth of August. One of the prisoners discovered the apparition and his fellows in bondage were severely frightened by the spirit."
—*Leadville Daily Herald, January 1, 1882*

* * * * * * *

- Courthouse-1882

For more than 60 years, Lake County's original courthouse stood streetside with the spirit-haunted jail attached on the west. Demolished after a fire gutted the structure, a 1950s-vintage building now stands in its place and contains county offices, jail and a few visiting astrals from another time.
Denver Public Library Western History Collection, #00300872.

* * * * * * *

"That ghost has been frightening the cook at the city jail again. It should be locked up in a dungeon. It was very naughty in its lifetime and death does not seem to have benefited it much."

—*Leadville Daily Herald, December 5, 1884*

* * * * * * *

'STRING ME UP AND WHIP ME'

As coincidence would have it, the location and physical configuration of the replacement jail was nearly identical to that of the original Leadville bastile. Early suicides and the surreal events they set in motion served up a buffet of uncanny events that spanned more than 12 decades.

In 1884, Upper Chestnut Street was home to a barmaid named Minnie, at least until the night she was arrested for drunkenness and led away to the jailhouse. The next morning, waking up behind bars, hung over and despondent from the penalties of the riotous life she was leading, Minnie procured a bottle of sulfate of morphia with the intention of putting an end to her tribulations. Quaffing a fatal dose of the deadly medicine, she lay undiscovered, sinking deeper into the throes of death until someone noticed her on the bed, barely breathing. Medical help arrived too late and Minnie put off mortality inside the dismal cell. No one claimed her body and two days later it was committed to the stony ground of the Potter's field.

Remorseful even in death, Miss Minnie's troubled spirit soon drifted back to the women's lockup, where it petrified the inmates by peering through the door of the death cell or standing, wistful and pale in the corridor outside.

One year later, the men's jail acquired a restless spirit of its own, and an 1884 edition of the Leadville Evening Chronicle detailed the eerie history of Cell No. 8.

"The prisoners in the county jail are kept in a sort of huge rectangular iron cage inside of which cells are built of metal plates. Around them and between the cage wall runs a corridor, and no matter how full the jail is, there is always one cell empty—No. 8. It is impossible to keep prisoners in it; at present the officers have ceased to try, and it stands empty and idle, an evidence of the truth of a very remarkable story."

Several years earlier, during Sheriff Tucker's term in office, a prisoner hung himself in No. 8. Alone at the time of the suicide, he was found dead the next morning dangling from a rope knotted around a bolt in the ceiling. For a short time, the cell was unused but the first man put into it screamed out in the middle of the night, begging the jailer to put him elsewhere. The terrified inmate shook with fear, saying that a corpse with a bruise around its neck crawled into the bunk with him. Nobody believed the tale and eventually a new prisoner was assigned to the cell. In the middle of the night the new man's screech woke the sleeping inmates. The turnkey listened as the man begged to be let out of the unholy compartment.

A dozen more prisoners were assigned to the chamber, each having the same experience. Their stories differed somewhat, but no one ever succeeded in passing the entire night in the haunted jail cell.

At least one of these inmates looks terrified at the prospect of encountering phantom felons in his jail cell, as caricatured by an artist in a 1918 edition of the San Juan Prospector. Prisons, jails and other lockups own a well-deserved reputation for being haunted, and those in Leadville were no exception.

* * * * * * *

"Since Sheriff Becker's regime, there have been several times, at periods of great crowding, prisoners were placed in the cell," an 1884 newspaper said. "They always had to be removed before morning. Some time ago, a big Englishman named Manning was arrested. He was a rough bully and gave the officers no end to trouble by his insubordination."

One evening, after an especially violent episode, Manning was clapped in Cell No. 8. Just after midnight, Jailor Letchmeyer heard a terrified yell, and unlocking the outside door, he went and looked into the Englishman's cell. He saw Manning's pale, sweating face peering from behind the bars, eyes nearly jumping from their sockets.

"For God's sake, jailor, let me out of here!" he told the turnkey. "String me up and whip me if you want to, but don't leave me here!"

Inquiring as to what was the matter, Letchmeyer listened as Manning said with chattering teeth, "Don't talk, but let me out! I'm going crazy in here!"

The custodian placed him in his old cell and the burly

Britisher caused no further trouble. After he calmed down, Manning said he was awakened by the touch of a clammy hand on his face. Staring up at the ceiling, he saw a ghastly glowing corpse dangling above him.

Another inmate named Hoyt was accidentally placed in the haunted cell but he had to be removed during the night, prostrated with fear, from which he finally recovered after several weeks. He explained how he awoke to the sight of a man with a rope around his neck standing in the middle of the cell and tying the noose to the ceiling. Speechless with terror at the sight of the suicidal prelude, Hoyt finally uttered a shriek that brought the jailor running to investigate the cause.

"The last victim of Cell No. 8 was Tom Collins, the incorrigible who was recently locked up on a charge of grand larceny," the newspaper reported. "He was there, and at the city jail, violent and unmanageable, and some of Manning's medicine given to him. He screamed for help, telling the same story as the others." Following the episode, Collins would go nowhere near the cell, even during the daytime.

Sheriff's employees agreed that the jail was full of strange noises and unnerving sounds. Jailor Letchmeyer said it was impossible to keep a revolver loaded during the night. He said he would be awakened from a nap to find that the pistol contained only empty shells. These manifestations, along with many others, equally strange, were repeated dozens of times in the old jail.

* * * * * *

"There are ghosts and spirits, and that is the end of it."
—*Leadville Daily & Evening Chronicle, September 12, 1892*

* * * * * *

GLOSSARY OF MINING TERMS

ADIT - *Horizontal excavation or passage into the earth.*

BONANZA POCKET - *Naturally occurring underground hollow areas of varying size whose sides are encrusted with pure gold, silver or extremely rich ore.*

BREAST - *In mining terms, the ore exposed on the face of a drift or crosscut.*

CARBONATE - *Type of ore containing carbonic acid and lead.*

CLAIM - *Space of ground located and worked under mining law.*

CRIBBING - *Timber or plank lining of a shaft that confines a wall of rock.*

CROSSCUT - *Opening of variable length generally running cross-course from a drift.*

DIGGINGS - *Name applied to placers that are being worked.*

DRIFT - *Horizontal passage underground.*

DUMP - *Place for deposit of tailings or waste rock.*

FACE OF THE DRIFT - *Rock exposed by blasting at the end of a drift.*

GIANT POWDER - *Dynamite*

GRUBSTAKE - *Provisions and food given in exchange for prospecting services.*

HARDROCKER - *Miner who works to extract valuable minerals from solid rock, as opposed to a placer miner, who digs for riches in loose earth and stream deposits.*

HEADFRAME - *Timber or metal frame standing above a mine shaft and supporting cables and other hoisting equipment.*

LAGGING - *Timbers over and upon the sides of a drift.*

MANWAY- *Shaft compartment containing ladders and platforms through which miners travel to and from the underground workings of a mine.*

MISSED HOLE-*Drill hole containing unexploded dynamite following blasting.*

MUCKING- *Loading dirt and loose rock into an ore car or bucket.*

PLACER- *Gravelly place where gold is found.*

PROSPECT HOLE- *Crater-like excavation formed after locating a likely spot to dig. If paying ore was found, it became a mine. Otherwise, it was abandoned.*

SHAFT COLLAR- *Opening of a shaft at the point where it enters the ground.*

SINGLE JACKING- *Drilling method in which a miner uses a hammer in one hand and a sharpened steel bit in the other.*

SPIT A FUSE- *Ignite a dynamite fuse using matches or a candle, whereupon it will appear to "spit" sparks.*

STOPE- *Room-like excavation into the side of the drift.*

SULFIDE- *Type of ore containing sulfur and one or more metals*

TRAMMER- *Mine employee whose primary job was to move ore cars along the drift between the ore face and the shaft.*

UPRAISE- *Excavation of small diameter in an upward direction.*

VEIN- *Aggregations of mineral matter in fissures of rocks.*

WINZE- *Small vertical shaft sunk from one drift to another.*

NEWSPAPER SOURCES

Aspen Daily Chronicle
Aspen Democrat
Aspen Tribune
Bayfield Blade
Boulder Daily Camera
Boulder News and Courier
Breckenridge Bulletin
Buena Vista Democrat
Canon City Record
Carbonate Chronicle
Carbonate Weekly Chronicle
Castle Rock Journal
Colorado Miner
Colorado Springs Gazette
Colorado Transcript
Creede Candle
Daily Chronicle
Daily Register Call
Denver Times
Dolores News
Durango Democrat
Eagle County Blade
Eagle Valley Enterprise
Elbert County Banner
Fairplay Flume
Fort Collins Courier
Georgetown Courier
La Plata Miner
Las Animas Leader
Leadville Daily Democrat
Leadville Daily & Evening Chronicle
Leadville Eclipse
Leadville Evening Chronicle
Leadville Weekly Chronicle
Leadville News
Leadville News-Dispatch
Leadville Reveille
Leadville Times
Longmont Ledger
Mancos Times Tribune
Morning Times
New York Times
Oak Creek Times
Rocky Mountain News
Rocky Mountain Sun
Saguache Chronicle
San Juan Prospector
Silverton Standard
Solid Muldoon
Stuart Chronicle
Summit County Journal
Telluride Daily Journal
Telluride Journal
White Pine Cone

SOURCES

Akers, Carl. Carl Akers' Colorado, Boulder, Colorado: Johnson Books, 1975

Baskins, O.L. & Co. History of the Arkansas Valley, Colorado, Chicago, Illinois: Historical Publishers, 1881

Blair, Edward. Leadville—Colorado's Magic City, Boulder, Colorado: Pruett Publishing Co., 1980

Davis, Carlyle Channing. Olden Times in Colorado, Los Angeles, California: The Phillips Publishing Co., 1936

Elder, Robert L. The St. Kevin Mine, monograph

Emmons, S.F., Irving, J.D., Laughlin, G.F. Geology and Ore Deposits of the Leadville Mining District, United States Government Printing Office, 1927

Fritz, Percy Stanley. Colorado-The Centennial State, New York: Prentice Hall, 1941

Griswold, Don L. and Jean Harvey. History of Leadville and Lake County, Colorado, Colorado Historical Society and University Press of Colorado, 1993

Mountain Diggings- Vol. 13, 1983

Paul, Wolfgang. Mining Lore-An Illustrated Composition and Documentary Compilation with Emphasis on the Spirit and History of Mining, Portland, Oregon: Morris Printing Co., 1970
Scribner's Monthly-Vol. 18, No. 6, October 1879

Smith, Duane A. Colorado Mining, A Photographic History, Albuquerque, New Mexico: University of New Mexico Press, 1977

Spooks, Spectres and Apparitions in Mining, Mining Journal, May 30, 1937, Vol. 21

Stone, Wilbur Fiske. History of Colorado, Vol. 1, Chicago, Illinois: The S.J. Clarke Publishing Co., 1918

The Illustrated London News- May 28, 1881

Wolle, Muriel Sibell. Stampede to Timberline—The Ghost Towns and Mining Camps of Colorado, Athens, Ohio: Swallow Press, 1949

ABOUT THE AUTHOR

Roger Pretti, a lifelong resident of Colorado, has a deep love of the state and its history. With family ties that extend back to 1880s Leadville, the Upper Arkansas Valley and its mining legacy holds a particular fascination for the author.

For many years, Pretti worked as the writer and part-time editor for the Leadville Chronicle, reporting local news and authoring dozens of feature articles about mining, historical personalities and life in the Cloud City during Victorian times. Intimately familiar with the town and the 16-square mile Leadville Mining District, Pretti has guided numerous mining and ghost tours of the area. He also is an authority on hundreds of the lesser-known but fascinating characters buried in Evergreen Cemetery.

Building upon a lifetime of personal paranormal experiences, many of which took place in Leadville, the author enjoys a strong connection to Leadville ghost lore. An archeologist, world traveler, cat lover and paranormal investigator, Pretti is often found exploring the hidden corners of the Centennial State.

BY THE SAME AUTHOR

Mining, Mayhem and Other Carbonate Excitements: Tales from a Carbonate Camp Called Leadville